158.1

Coaching

The key to unlocking your potential

Beache Key Publication

First published In 2003 by
Beache Key Publications
38 Ashton Avenue
Knocklyon
Dublin 16

© Carmel Wynne 2003

ISBN 0 - 9546643 - 0 - 2

A CIP record for this title is available
from the British Library

Cover design by Artwerk Ltd.
Printed In Ireland by ColourBooks
Baldoyle Industrial Estate, Dublin 13

Acknowledgements

This work has been undertaken with the encouragement of many people. First I would like to thank Colm for his support, patience, editing and hard work. Your loving support and belief in how I work encourages me to take risks and do things I never believed I could do. I'm so aware of how helpful it is when you challenge me to 'go for it.' I'm wondering if you know how I value and appreciate your help and how coaching can help to stop procrastination. Thank you for being my husband and friend.

I appreciate the help my daughter Deirdre-Anne Wynne-Robinson gave by reading the proofs of this book. I value your integrity. Your honest feedback on the manuscript has helped me greatly.

So many other family members and friends love me and have played a role in encouraging me to expand my horizons. There are so many people that I want to thank. To list their individual names would take a book. Thank you to my extended family, my wonderful friends, colleagues, clients and students.

I'd like to thank Mary Stewart, Principal of St. Pius X Primary School, Templeogue, Dublin and teacher Mary Ryan. A very special work of thanks to the 5th class pupils who gave me permission to tell adults that making a list of values is child's play and can be done by anyone.

I am very blessed to have benefited from the wisdom and guidance of teachers and mentors to whom I owe a huge debt of gratitude. I particularly want to express my gratitude to John Callanan S.J., and Mary Kavanagh. I pay tribute to Dick McHugh S.J., Ph. D., Dr. Sean Collins, Rhoda Draper and Professor Donal Hollywood who have played such a huge role in my recovery from the trauma of breast cancer.

My personal coach Tom Creaven has been immensely encouraging and challenging. Thank you to all the participants on seminars, workshops and conferences. Thank you to the many who brought challenging agendas that caused me to be creative. I have borrowed concepts, materials and outlines from many disciplines that I have adapted, altered and changed. I am no longer sure of the original authorship of many of the exercises I now use. Forgive me if I have bastardised your material.

I want to thank James for being a calm force during hectic mealtime preparation, to Mark for cooking and John for his computer expertise in keeping the website up to date and teaching me that I can overcome my fears of technology.

I am delighted to name my other daughters Aileen and Aoife-Marie. You know that I love you and am so proud that you have grown into lovely independent young women and my loving friends.

And finally I want to give thanks for the gift of my faith; for the spiritual teachers who have lighted the path as I was challenged to have courage and risk moving out into the unknown; the 'Awareness' teachings of Anthony de Mello S.J. changed my life for the better. He said that 'Spirituality is that which succeeds in bringing one to inner transformation.'

AUTHOR'S NOTES

In order to avoid the awkwardness of 's/he'. 'his or her' and any other such pronoun complications, throughout the text the client will be referred to as 'he' and the Life Coach as 'she' unless the context clearly requires gender specificity.

The terms Life, Business, Personal and Professional Coach are interchangeable. As the terms Life Coach, Life and Business Coach , Professional Coaching and Personal Coaching are all interchangeable and it is clumsy to use all four, I will use the term 'Life Coach' except where specificity demands otherwise.

This book is dedicated to my daughter Niamh with love and appreciation. Thank you for you so generously taking on the roles of organiser, secretary, cook, cleaner and chauffeur. Thank you for being a wonderful daughter and a beautiful person.

CONTENTS

INTRODUCTION

> 'Perhaps real individual failure lies in the squandering of potentiality, a volitional waste of one's ability. If you paint signs when you could paint sunsets, invent jingles when you might compose symphonies, forgoing eventual achievement in favour of instant reward, that may be regarded as personal failure'.
>
> **Bob Monkhouse.**

The key to unlocking your potential is rooted in what you believe. Coaching will help you to discover how to unlock the many inner resources that lie dormant and unused in you because you fail to recognise that they are there.

If you are curious about how coaching gets such quick results and why it is hailed as the 21st century fast track to success you will find the answers between the covers of this book. Learn how to decide on positive goals, make detailed plans for the outcome you want and draw up a blueprint for how to achieve the success you desire.

The secret of successful coaching is in the relationship that develops between the coach and the client. The motivational power of working with an encouraging, interested coach to keep you on track cannot be overestimated. A problem with any book that invites you to become your own coach is that one vital ingredient that is essential to the coaching process is missing – the live person who will challenge you to follow through on the plans that you make.

Coaching does not provide a magic formula for success. The client's willingness to undertake the work involved and be open to think and act in new ways is vital to a successful outcome. Commitment to action is necessary for progress.

The shops are full of self-help books that tell you how to change your life in seven days, become your own coach, transform your prospects, advance your career and bring balance to your life. They have catchy titles, are well written, based on documented research and full of practical advice on how to do whatever the title suggests.

If readers do exactly what the authors suggest, they experience the benefits of a change in thinking. Lives would be transformed permanently if readers were to take the advice and action suggested in these books. Many don't. Avid readers of self-help books have a desire for personal development but they find it difficult to tackle the work that is suggested. Some people simply read through exercises that require time and effort to complete. They decide that it is too much trouble to follow the recommendation of sitting down and writing answers. They do them mentally and experience small benefits but few experience the major life-changes that are promised.

Coaching helps people who say they want change but rationalise their failure to take action by saying things like 'I'm too old' or 'I lack educational qualifications.' These are self-limiting beliefs that create obstacles to success. When they are challenged they rarely stand up to scrutiny. Did you know that in the United States the Vice Presidents of most of the top companies have either a Masters or Ph.D. degree but almost none of their bosses, the Chief Executive Officers, have university qualifications?

An author can give you guidelines on what action you must take to achieve the outcome you desire. She can teach you to understand the process of setting positive goals and help you discover the impact that achieving them will have on other aspects of your life. The work in changing your beliefs and attitude you will have to do for yourself.

I am glad that you have picked up this book. In it you will find an explanation of what coaching is and how the process works. You will benefit from the goal setting exercises, skill building techniques and learn how to think in positive ways that enhance self-esteem and build self-belief. The benefits you will get from reading this book will be in direct proportion to the time and effort you put into engaging with the exercises.

The limitation of this self-help book is that the written word can inspire good intentions in the reader but it cannot encourage you when you feel disappointed with a lack of progress or challenge you to find a way forward when you feel stuck or mirror back unhelpful thinking that limits your options for achievement.

I know you will benefit from working through the exercises I use with clients. When you understand goal setting, how to reframe and think in a positive way and what stops you from taking action you have made good progress. The positive benefits of doing the exercises are easy to measure. They literally help you change your mind.

The results of becoming aware of your own habitual put-downs and learning how to stop negative thinking are immediate. Your outlook on life is changed for the better. You move from the black and white, either/or thinking that limits choices and find limitless possibilities for positive change.

Almost everyone is limited by his own belief system rather like the two guys who looked out through prison bars; one saw mud and the other saw stars. In one-to-one coaching the client is challenged to expand his horizons. It's the difference between focusing on the obstacles that block achievement and lifting your gaze to see new horizons and identify new possibilities.

You would not believe how many people are unaware of what a negative outlook they have on life. As you work through some of the exercises in this book you may find that your approach is less positive than you realised. When I write about the exercises I will tell you what a reader can do on his own. I also explain the limitations of working without a coach.

Everyone needs to be challenged to break out of the prison of self-imposed limitations that narrow vision and diminish dreams. This book will provide that challenge but it may not be enough. If you are not making progress you will benefit from a relationship with a coach who is committed to your goals and who will challenge you to stay on track.

Readers will have many different approaches to self-help and personal development. Some are self-starters who find it easy to plan, are focused and see projects through from start to finish. They will find this book invaluable. Others are what I call 'Beginning self-starters.' They start off with good intentions and begin with great enthusiasm but tend to get bogged down in projects. Halfway through they get tired, find the effort too much and leave the book aside.

They know only too well the limitations of a self-help book. Procrastinators dip into self-help books, intend to read them properly and put off getting started. Then they go out and buy other books to help them understand why they defer and delay.

I give you lots of theory and practical exercises to help you have positive goals. I alert you to self-sabotage, and the inner dialogue that de-motivates, discourages and stops achievement. I write about building self-esteem and the importance of being honest with oneself.

Honesty is at the root of every effective coaching relationship. I do not make false promises. I spell out that this book has one big limitation. The personal challenge to move readers out of their comfort zones is missing. I cannot look you in the eye and challenge you to think in a different way when you put yourself down or limit your choices. For that you will need to build a relationship with a Life Coach who is committed to your goals and challenges you to be your very best.

Reading this book will not miraculously empower you to reach your potential. I hope it will motivate you to 'Gaze at the stars' and use the information that gives you the tools for the self-knowledge that will empower you to be whatever you want to be and to achieve your dream. I want you to share my confidence that you can be and do anything you believe is possible.

You hold the key to transforming your thinking and finding creative ways to achieving your potential. Working with a coach will help you find the resources to achieve success easily, elegantly and beautifully.

Definition of Success: 'Doing what you would be doing for free but doing it well enough that people will pay you'.

                                                    QUENTIN REYNOLDS.

CHAPTER 1

BASICS OF GOAL SETTING

IN THIS CHAPTER:

- **Support makes a difference.**
- **Expectations lead to success and failure.**
- **Perceptions about success.**
- **SMARTO.**

A woman who was forever complaining that she was unable to achieve her potential went to see a famous guru. 'Life is unfair,' she complained.

'I have been deprived of so many opportunities because I was born a women.'

The guru said 'It is you who make your destiny.'

'But surely I am not responsible for being born a woman?'

'Being born a woman isn't destiny. That is fate. Destiny is how you accept your womanhood and what you do with it.'

MOTIVATION TO GET WHAT YOU WANT

Every January millions of people make New Year resolutions. They set out to take exercise, lose weight, spend more time with the family or whatever. Using the language of coaching their goals are specific, achievable, realistic and have a time frame. I don't need to tell you that within a few weeks many of those well-intentioned people will have abandoned their goals.

Why do so many people fail to carry out their good intentions? There is no one simple answer because people have all sorts of reasons for what they do. Men and women have different ways of looking at success and failure. Some people are disappointed when they break their resolutions, others have expectations that they will fail. They were never really motivated to put in the effort to succeed.

Isn't it strange that some people set themselves up for failure? Every year they make resolutions with the expectation that the resolutions won't last. Then it becomes a self-fulfilling prophecy. It is widely accepted that people live up to their own expectations. They have beliefs that influence how they think and what they achieve or fail to achieve.

Do you realise how powerful your beliefs are? When you believe you can do something you are right. When you tell yourself that you won't succeed you are right too. If people expect failure, that is what they get.

Society is very ready to make simplistic judgements. How often do you hear that those who do not succeed in life lack drive or motivation or are weak-willed? All of these judgements are inaccurate. They are also unhelpful.

Many well-intentioned people abandon hopes of achieving outcomes that are far more serious than a new year's resolution. It is important for them to succeed. They try, they put in the work and despite their best efforts success eludes them. They attempt something else and it doesn't work out. As a consequence of repeated disappointments they form beliefs about themselves that discourage them from taking risks and as a result they never reach their potential.

Life experience teaches one person that he is unlikely to achieve success. Another person with similar experiences will have a different way of looking at life. His attitude when things don't work out as he planned is to find out what doesn't work and then try something else. How is it that one person will be challenged to seek creative solutions to a problem that caused another to despair?

Happily there is help now available for people who need support to achieve a goal that is important to them. It has become popular and trendy to work with a Life Coach who will support her client in the planning and achieving of his goals. There is no doubt that it is easier to follow through on a project when someone is on your side encouraging you to persist in your efforts. It's amazing how someone having faith in your ability to succeed will bring out the best in you.

People who cannot achieve something on their own can often be very successful when they join a group with the same focus. Feeling supported in one's efforts to change makes a huge difference. Self-help groups offer the support and understanding that empowers people to successfully deal with issues like weight loss and various forms of addictions.

People who decide to work with a Life Coach often achieve far more than they expect. They have a personal goal. They want an outcome that they believe they can achieve and they need support. Some have learned from painful experience that they get discouraged easily and give up. They know they cannot manage on their own without some outside challenge to keep them on track.

Other people come to coaching because they have seen how it helped someone they know. They watched the changes a friend or colleague made as a result of coaching. They believe the process works because they have seen someone who used to procrastinate change their behaviour and become organised in a matter of weeks; or heard how someone who was unemployed has started up a successful business. If it works for others why wouldn't it work for them?

In coaching as in everything else in life nothing breeds success like success. Clients who come to coaching on the recommendation of a friend usually arrive with the expectation that they have finally found a way to move forward. They are motivated to succeed and that is half the battle. Some come with unrealistic expectations about what coaching can do for them. One appointment with a coach is unlikely to produce magic long-term results.

QUICK FIX – A SHORT TERM SOLUTION

Most Life Coaches take a holistic approach and contract to see clients over a number of sessions. A small number do not. Some coaches have a very short-term problem solving approach to goal setting. They see a client for one session and deal with the specific issue that the client presents.

This one-stop approach is useful for the person who is preparing for an interview. The coach can make sure that he has taken the trouble to have up to date information about his prospective employers and advise him how to dress and present the right image for the job. She will check that he has a well set out curriculum vitae that presents his achievements in the best possible light.

For someone looking for direction on how to re-enter the workforce a one-off session is useful. There are fashions in the language and terminology that are used in the workplace. Somebody who has not worked for a couple of years may go for an interview and find they are unfamiliar with buzz words like;

- action learning,
- appraisals,
- self-management,
- thinking skills,
- goal setting,
- peer reviews.

A one-off session with a coach that brings them up to date with the jargon that is currently fashionable is useful.

There are a variety of ways to deliver coaching. Clients have varied commitments and for some a weekly telephone call with the client calling the coach works well. Others meet at set times and use e-mail to keep in contact between meetings. I prefer face-to-face sessions until the coaching relationship is well developed. I am writing about a longer term coaching relationship, which deals in a holistic way with the whole person.

Clients don't buy a packaged program. The client is a full partner in bringing balance and fulfilment as well as more success into his life. The coach will encourage new learning. You can look at any situation from many different perspectives. This simple strategy changes how you view any problem or difficulty.

At every meeting the coach will invite her client to report on the action he has taken. Action and learning are the two forces that combine to move the client's agenda forward. Reporting on progress he has made keeps him accountable for staying on the course he has mapped out for himself.

Parts of the early sessions cover issues like the client's life purpose or mission and his personal beliefs. It's easier to deal with sensitive matters like these when the coach and client are with each other in person.

People have different criteria when they measure success. What is highly valued and incredibly important for one person to achieve can be unappreciated and regarded as of little value to another.

The divorced wife of a rich man seeks the services of a coach because she cannot manage to live on €150,000 a year. Another client celebrates a pay increase that brings his salary up to €50,000 a year. His measure of wealth is that he feels rich on an annual income that is one third of the amount that has the divorced women feeling poverty stricken. It's not what a person has but how he reacts to what he has that makes him rich or poor, successful or a failure.

A WELL-FORMED OUTCOME

One of the many definitions of coaching is that it is 'a powerful alliance designed to forward and enhance the lifelong process of human learning, effectiveness and fulfilment.' When Neuro-Linguistic Programming (NLP) and coaching are used together even the most daunting goals become manageable. You can take almost any task and break it down into simple steps, chunk it down to basics and begin from the first action to be taken. The journey of a thousand miles begins with the first step. Take one step at a time and a project that seemed overwhelming becomes manageable. Your goal stops where your responsibility and power stop. For a well-formed outcome you must have the authority to initiate change.

Initiating positive change in how you think will have an immediate impact on how you feel. Positive thinking does not come easily but its effects are instantly recognisable. Most of us are not in a position to immediately change where we live or how we earn our living. We can instantly change our attitude to both and that is the difference that makes the difference. Coaching empowers clients to do the work that creates these positive changes.

It's incredible how quickly myths about coaching have proliferated. It is true that the majority of coaches invite the client to work with the SMARTO model of goal-setting. It has a well-deserved reputation for being immensely successful. It's a modern approach and is easy to follow but there is far more to coaching than simply setting goals. SMARTO is ideal for people who feel they are unfocused, need help to commit to a project or are poor time managers. It's a useful tool.

You may be familiar with the six characteristics. Each goal must be:

- Specific,
- Measurable,
- Achievable,
- Realistic,
- Timed,
- Owned.

It helps keep clients on track. The client states exactly what goal he wants to achieve and when he hopes to do so. He is invited to make sure that his outcome is realistic and is something that he is capable of achieving. He will want to decide on how he will measure the successful completion of his goal. 'Owned' means that it must be the client's own goal and not something other people want him to achieve.

SMARTO is an excellent tool to help clients get started. It is widely used because it motivates the client to come up with successful strategies for specific outcomes that he desires. Many people report that they radically improved their business prospects and career choices by using this approach to setting and achieving goals.

CHECKING EXPECTATIONS

It is important for clients to have realistic expectation of the commitment involved in the coaching relationship. When a client sets out to list the elements of a well-formed outcome the coach will invite him to think very clearly about all that is involved. In the process he will be challenged to broaden his horizons. Few clients are aware that when they achieve a goal they may have to deal with changes they had not anticipated.

I encourage all of my clients to take a long-term as well as a short-term approach to setting goals. Recognising success at each step of the process gives a sense that a project is moving forward. Success builds on success and is a great motivator to keep on with the work.

Some first-time clients feel excited when they sit down to use the SMARTO model to plan their goals. Others have already done this preliminary work. They realise that there is a lot more to goal setting than they first recognised. This is why they decide to work with a coach.

Clients rarely take time out to reflect on how getting their goal will have an impact on other areas of life. Some people come to the first coaching session expecting the coach to give them a plan of action that they will implement and 'Hey presto' they have their goal and life is wonderful. I'm sorry to tell you that coaching doesn't work in that way. If you are looking to make changes in your life or career you may be surprised at how much work you will be expected to undertake. A client can want an outcome that appears incredibly appealing to him. When he works with a coach he may find that goal is unwise because of how his life will change.

The main difference between clients who achieve and those who don't is a sense of purpose, passion or mission. Erma Bombeck said

'I always wanted to be somebody but I should have been more specific'. Nora Watson said, 'I think most of us are looking for a calling, not a job. Most of us have jobs that are too small for our spirit. Jobs are not big enough for people.'

In the coaching relationship you will be challenged to raise your expectations of yourself. You will be invited to move out of your comfort zones and reassess how effective are your current life strategies. In the process you will be invited to look at what is working in your life and what you want to change.

In order to achieve any goal you need an effective strategy that will bring all the key elements of your life and work together. You need to be clear and specific about what you want to do and why. A good beginning is to find what you love to do. Set out to make your work a labour of love. You will need to plan the steps you have to take, what resources you will need, and be very sure about the impact of a successful conclusion on yourself and others.

DREAM THE DREAM

You will need a specific plan for successfully completing each step. These are your short-term goals. I always ask my clients to 'Dream the dream.' I want them to have a strong internal representation of what they will feel when they achieve their final outcome. I invite them to forget about being realistic and to ignore any obstacle that might get in the way.

Let's say I am working with you. You want to change your career and work for yourself. I ask you 'How will your life be different when you are self-employed.' I invite you to dream the dream and see yourself as a successful man and to describe the scene to me.

- Where are you, indoors or out?
- What are you doing?

- What are your surroundings like?
- What have you achieved?
- How does this make you feel?
- Tell me more about how it is to have achieved this.

When a client paints a bright, vivid, colourful picture of his dream his enthusiasm is infectious. His motivation to achieve is strong and he has clarity about what he wants to do in the future. Once he is clear about what he wants his next task is to say how he will go about making the dream a reality.

The job of the coach is to invite the client to create the dream, look to see if it is realistic and then plan how he will achieve each step on the way to making the dream real. She will make sure that his plans are realistic, congruent with his values, beliefs and spirituality.

Many very gifted people fail to achieve their potential. They have ability and talent and what stops them is lack of self-belief. Let me briefly introduce you to a part of you that many coaches call 'The Gremlin.' That's the name we give to that little inner voice, the inner dialogue that is responsible for poor self-esteem.

Many people are not even aware of how they talk to themselves in their mind. They have no idea that they hold conversations with themselves. They are so familiar with their negative thoughts that they never stop to wonder where do they come from? They fail to recognise how they limit their own achievements. Negative self-talk has its origins in the past. Some psychologists compare this to having an internal tape playing 'Put-down' messages you heard in childhood.

You can refuse to replay childhood messages about not being good enough. A client needs to understands the negative impact of thoughts that discourage and sow doubt about his abilities. He can learn techniques to change his thinking. These are some of the discoveries that are made later in the coaching process.

COACHING SESSIONS

In every coaching session the client is challenged to move forward. He is invited to have aims for what he wants to achieve in each session. At the end of the session he will go away with a work plan and a clear framework for what he is to achieve before he meets his coach again.

During the session his coach will work with the client's long term goals. She will listen to his progress report of what happened to the work he committed to do between sessions. In that process the client will be challenged to give an account of how he worked to achieve the smaller goals that are the stepping stones to his successful long term outcome. His coach will give him honest feedback and challenge him to stay focused and on track.

SPECIFIC

It's easy to say 'What works for one person will, when done in the same way work for you.' The client needs to have a specific goal for a start. The strong motivation of the client is not the key element in a successful outcome. It's what he believes combined with how hard he works.

Think of a goal you would like to achieve?

Can you describe in detail how you feel about achieving this? If you can't you need to do more work. Remember that you are more likely to create what you believe in.

What are you aware of when you picture achieving the results you want?

In your fantasy of achieving your dream are you using all of your senses?

Do you see a life-size, moving picture in bright, vivid colours? Or do you make a small black and white or sepia toned snapshot image? If that's your image you need more clarity about what you want and why you believe this goal will benefit you.

It is important to picture what you want. Why? Your brain makes a mental representation, an image of any outcome you desire. The more vivid the picture you make the stronger its effect in motivating you. That is why the first step in SMARTO is so helpful. You want your specific goal to become the spur that will drive you towards the successful outcome you desire. As you work with this model you become clearer about the benefits you gain from achieving these goals.

MEASURABLE

Your coach cannot define or measure success for you. This is something that only you can do for yourself. A positive measure of success is whatever you decide. Make sure that whatever definition you choose will have positive consequences and encourage you to feel that you are moving towards your goals.

Some things you will need to think about are:
- How will you measure your successful outcome?
- What evidence will you use to define that you are successful?
- Will you use only your own feedback?
- Will you look for outside evaluation?
- How will you do that?
- What criteria will you use?

In this process coaching with a mentor is incredibly helpful. She can ask you;

- 'Will you focus only on completion targets or will you also recognise partial achievements?'
- 'For what purpose will you measure that?'

Finding the purpose for what you do is more important than most people recognise. Are you measuring your own efforts by your own standards? A mentoring coach will monitor how her client responds. You'd be surprised at how often the client is unconsciously influenced by voices from the past that either demand perfection or taunt with promises of failure. 'Don't do it at all if it's not done well'. I have talented clients who were told as children, 'You'll never amount to much'. We will deal with how to cope with this later.

The coach knows when to ask the curious questions that will challenge the client to ask more of himself. She will encourage him to push out the boundaries and to become his best self. You cannot find that challenge in the pages of a book.

When I work with a client I want to encourage him to recognise personal achievements. If he says, 'I tried hard and did better than yesterday,' I want that to count as a measurable success. It's so important for a client to recognise small victories.

Think about it this way. When you give yourself credit for trying you're tuned in to a positive mindset. Big successes are built on smaller ones. In the beginning it is important that a client measures success around goals that he can initiate and maintain himself. Say you have worthwhile goals for project work that involves others. Make sure you are specific about the part of the project you control. That is where you own the goal and measure success.

ACHIEVABLE

The main difference between people who achieve great things and those who don't is a sense of mission that gives their life purpose and meaning. Ted Turner, founder of CNN, brought cable televisions news to the world. He created the Goodwill Games which lost eighty million dollars in 1986 and 1990. He explained that because television news is so powerful he had a responsibility not to make a lot of money but to have an influence on the world in which we live. His motivating vision is a huge almost unachievable dream – he wants peace on earth.

Make sure that your goal is worth achieving as well as being achievable. Is your outcome specific and stated in a way that you can get it yourself? Will achieving this goal enhance your life? Have you decided on how you will measure success? Do you have a vivid picture of what you will see and hear and feel as you achieve each step on the way to your final outcome? Will you achieve your goal no matter what other people do?

To achieve any goal you need to make an action plan.
- What you will do in order to achieve your goal?
- Make your plan very detailed. Plan it out step by step.
- What is the first thing you will do?
- What if any resources do you want?
- When will you complete step one?

Do this for every step. Decide to monitor success based on achieving each step on the way to the ultimate goal. Ask yourself questions like 'When, where and with whom do I want each goal?' You may find that you only want a certain goal in a very specific situation or with only certain people. You may want a successful outcome in some contexts and not in others.

Rewording your goal can help. As you become clearer about what you intend to achieve you may find that you need to go back to step one and rethink your goal. Feel free to do so. Isn't it wonderful that SMARTO is helping you to be clearer about what you desire?

Later in the book I will look at how we allow negative self-talk to discourage us. It is so easy to ignore small success and feel disappointed with what we judge as a lack of progress. Becoming aware of little achievements gives us a positive outlook. It sensitises us and we become more aware of how to let go of negative thinking.

REALISTIC

You understand that sometimes you may have to restrict a goal that depends on others and focus on the part of the outcome that you can achieve yourself. For example to write a book is achievable. So setting out to write a book is an achievable and realistic goal. To write a world best seller is not a realistic goal. You have little control over how it will be marketed or sold. Unless you have special expertise in marketing the only part you fully control is writing the book.

Setting a realistic goal involves more than a wish list. It takes more than talent for an unknown author to get a book published. It takes hard work and determination and self-belief. The author may need to get an agent or employ other expertise in the process. If someone has done something even once then it is possible for other people to do the same thing depending on merit and market forces.

'I want to organise my study and put the papers in files today' sounds achievable. Whether it is realistic or not will depend on other factors. The motivation of the client is always important.

Before you can say the goal is realistic you would need to look at the quantity of paper, the number of files, storage capacity and find if any action is to be taken before filing. These are all relevant questions as to how realistic is your outcome.

A sixty years old woman who sets herself the goal of becoming a brain surgeon is hardly setting a realistic goal. Your outcome must be realistic as well as achievable. It is not enough to have half-baked ideas or vague plans about what you would like to happen. You want to be able to make it happen.

It's wonderful to have the theory that you create a powerful representation of what success means for you and that will bring the image and feelings alive. Seeing, hearing and feeling does not happen in isolation or in a vacuum. It has to be in some context where you take responsibility for your part in bringing this plan to fruition. The following questions will help you clarify if you are being realistic:

The all-important 'W' questions are a wonderful tool for clarity;

- What is my goal?
- What steps must I take to achieve this?
- Where do I want this goal?
- When do I want this goal?
- With whom do I want to have this goal?
- When will I achieve this?

Your desired outcome needs to be imagined in a real-life context. You will probably find that there are some goals that you only want at certain times and only with a number of people. This is why it is so important to spend time on creating positive goals and being realistic about the context in which you want them and when you might not want them.

TIMED

Setting out a realistic timeframe is the easiest part of the
SMARTO model. Go over the list you made of each step on the
way to achieving your goal. Put a completion date on each. It is
helpful to set a timeframe even if it is only a rough guideline.
Being flexible and free to change as you progress is an intelligent
response. When you are specific about the goal you want you may
find that you will have a number of short-term goals that are steps
on the way to the long-term or ultimate goal.

OWNED

Clients have to be clear that they are not fulfilling other people's
goals. 'I want to see my sons in college, working hard and
enjoying academic success' may be some mother's dream but it is
not an owned goal. 'I want to support my children with their
tuition fees in college and I will open a savings account for that
purpose' is a healthier outcome because she controls it.

WORKING WITH A LIFE COACH

Learning how to use SMARTO to set specific, measurable,
achievable, realistic, timed and owned goals does not explain why
coaching is so effective and gives such quick results. That is simply
the beginning of the process. It's barely the tip of the iceberg.

The benefits of working with a Life Coach have to be experienced
to be understood. The coach offers encouragement, support, and
challenge. I don't mean to be funny and I don't want to make
things complicated but do you have any idea about what giving
'Support, encouragement and challenge' means?

ENCOURAGEMENT

When a client is hard on himself he needs to be challenged about
how he thinks. When someone uses an unrealistic measure of

success he needs to be invited to think in a different way. In other words he needs to learn how to reframe his measure of success.

There is no formula for doing this. 'I don't accept that you are a failure if you don't immediately achieve what you set out to do' may sound encouraging to one person and feel like a put-down to another. She will encourage the client to think positively. How success is measured is very personal.

When I know a client's background and motivation I can encourage him to measure success in a way that will motivate him to persist. I cannot do that with readers. The best I can do is suggest how you might challenge yourself.

You decide on what is success for you. Focus on what will help you feel that what you are achieving can be measured. If you have to delegate parts of a project you can influence the outcome but you cannot control how others perform. Bear that in mind when you measure success.

When you have a positive outlook you will deal with any problems that arise. Why? Because you will see opportunities to be creative where another person might feel stuck. There will be times when things will not work out according to plan. Your attitude will decide how you respond to setbacks. It's your decision whether they are measured as successes, failures or learning opportunities.

If you were to substitute the word 'Feedback' for 'Failure' would that change your perception? Is learning what doesn't work useful? Is it helpful? Does it challenge you to rethink how you measure failure? I always work in the context that the client knows the answers. He just needs to be asked the challenging questions to let them emerge.

There are many ways of supporting someone. I can give him money, I can speak to him in a positive way, I can hold him up if he is drunk, I can telephone to say I'm thinking of him. Words like 'Encouragement' and 'Challenge' also have a variety of different meaning. You probably never thought of this before but you give words a meaning.

When you read words you have a response to what you read. Many clients baulk when they are invited to say how they feel. I remember working with one man who initially hated to be asked about his feelings. He used to say things like, 'I don't know. I don't have any feelings.' I disagreed. I knew that while he was dead to his feelings he was missing out on the positive energy that would increase his motivation and commitment to achieving his goals.

He asked me to make him a list of feeling words so that he could go away and think about them. Being an experienced coach I did not point out the contradiction to him. I waited for him to discover it himself and in time he made the connection. Sensitive to his discomfort with the word 'Feelings' I changed how I communicated. I used different words with him to help him find a response.

The meaning of communication is the response you get. If you are not getting the response you want you change your communication and keep changing it until you get the response you desire. I changed what I said and he responded positively.

Instead of asking him to get in touch with his feelings I suggested that, 'Today I want to work with you on expressing your goals in specific, sensory terms. It's a way of tuning your neurology and to in effect rehearse the links your brain needs to make in order to keep you highly motivated. Vivid sensory representation of your desired outcome will set up a sequence of neural associations that steer you from internal experience to external reality. To do this you will want to work on writing down your internal representations.'

This worked brilliantly with this client. If I used that language with someone else they may have felt patronised or put-down by those words.

A caring mentor will always begin working with a client where he is at and then find ways to get him to move forward. My client had a mental block about the word 'Feelings.' He felt inadequate to describe his internal experience. I discarded questions that he felt uncomfortable answering, used different terminology and he found the answers. He also taught me a lesson that has proved valuable with other clients. Many clients who feel intimidated when asked 'How do you feel?' are very happy to answer when asked 'What's your response to that?'

Some clients have a problem distinguishing between thoughts and feelings. There is a very simple way to recognise which is which. If you can put 'I think' in front of the word and it is grammatically incorrect it is a feeling. For example, put 'I think' in front of 'Annoyed,' 'Sad,' 'Happy,' 'Angry' or 'Frustrated.' It is not grammatical so you have found words that describe feelings.

This is important to understand because it helps explain the power of the coaching relationship. People naturally shy away from issues and situations that make them feel uncomfortable. Rather than face the discomfort some people abandon their goals. They have good reasons for that decision. The benefit of working with a coach is that she will challenge the client to move out of his comfort zones and encourage him to believe that he will have the support he needs when so doing.

The coach does not perform miracles. She guides a process that supports and encourages the client as he finds strategies to achieve what he wants. She invites him to do what is necessary to become the best that he can be. She encourages him to identify his beliefs and values and to reflect on whether his way of life fits in with them. The process is life-changing but not miraculous.

SMARTO

When doing any of the exercises in this book you may find it helpful to write at length about your response to a question. Having clarified your thoughts, summarise your answer in one sentence.

Identify one goal you want to achieve in each of these areas - career, finance and personal development.

Career _____

_____

In what context do you want this?

Are there times when you don't want the outcome?

Is it sensory specific? Are you clear about how you want to feel and what sights and sounds you will be aware of when you get this outcome?

What steps will you take to achieve this goal?

Finance _____

_____

In what context do you want this?

Are there times when you don't want the outcome?

Is it sensory specific? Are you clear about how you want to feel and what sights and sounds you will be aware of when you get this outcome?

What steps will you take to achieve this goal?

Personal development_____

_____

In what context do you want this?

Are there times when you don't want the outcome?

Is it sensory specific? Are you clear about how you want to feel and what sights and sounds you will be aware of when you get this outcome?

What steps will you take to achieve this goal

Using the SMARTO model of goal setting check that each goal is specific.

- How will you measure success?
- When will you do to achieve this goal?
- What is your evidence for saying it is realistic?
- What date will you start working towards the goal?
- What date will you achieve your goal?
- Is this owned by you?

Now you understand the basics of setting goals. Well done!

SUMMARY

- You live up to your own expectations.
- SMARTO.
- Dream the dream.
- Focus on the outcome you can achieve

'The real voyage of discovery consists not in seeking new landscapes but in having new eyes'.

MARCEL PROUST.

CHAPTER 2

WHAT'S IT ALL ABOUT?

IN THIS CHAPTER:

- **How does it work?**
- **Are there professional standards?**
- **Is it a trendy fad?**
- **Why the confusion?**
- **Who needs a coach?**

> 'My goal and mission in life reflects who I am.
> It defines how I use my inner abilities.
> And it guides how I act in the world.'
> Charles Faulkner NLP Comprehensive.

PHENOMENOM OR FAD?

People ask, 'What is coaching?' 'What will a coach do for me?'
Coaching is such a new profession that they want to know if there
is a difference between Personal/Professional Coaching and Life
and Business Coaching?' If you look up 'coach' in the New
Oxford Dictionary you will find it defined as, 'A single decker bus,'
'A railway carriage' and 'An instructor or trainer in sports.'

My definition of a Coach is, 'A person who works in a mentoring
role with a client who wants to initiate change in one or more
areas of his life.' The same dictionary defines 'Mentor' as 'An
experienced and trusted adviser: he was her friend and mentor.'

All coaches work to help the client unlock his potential and give support in the planning and implementation stages of personal and career goals. Clients who come for one-to-one coaching have varied backgrounds. Some have academic backgrounds and marketable skills. Others are on a career break and testing the market place. Others still may have been unemployed and are trying to get back into the workforce. Coaching is just as useful for a stay-at home-parent who is seeking a new challenge as it is for a top-ranking manager.

Most of the people who train as Life Coaches are already highly skilled creative, professional people. Many are seeking a career change and when they are qualified specialise in an area in which they already have professional experience and expertise. Some training programmes assign a qualified Life Coach to work with trainees. Others have the participants in training coach each other as part of their training.

Coaching is a holistic process that deals with all aspects of a client's life. Many people focus on developing their career and are so busy that they fail to care for their general wellbeing. The goal of a Life Coach is to help the client unlock his potential in whatever ways challenge and encourage him to move forward and have balance in every area of his life. I work with my clients on the basis that they have resources and when they use them they can achieve realistic goals.

There is no denying that there are sceptics who fear that coaching is another trendy fad that will entice vulnerable and inadequate people to be parted from money they can ill afford. The speed with which Life Coaching has become popular is a measure of how well the process works.

Is it any wonder that there is much confusion about what exactly coaching is and how the process of working one-to-one with a coach can help. It is difficult to say how a coach will work with a client because so much depends on the client and how willing he is to put in hard work. His results will be influenced by his motivation to succeed.

In Ireland the word 'Coaching' is used to describe anything from a 'One-off' face-to-face session to a contract for regular meetings at an agreed venue for a set period of time. Some people who formerly called themselves Trainers now use the term Coach.

The terms Life & Business Coach and Personal/Professional Coach are interchangeable. Executive Coaching covers a number of different and varied approaches. At the upper end of the market a small number of firms include Executive Coaching with the company car and platinum credit card as perks of the job.

Working with a coach the client learns that he can change his thinking by learning to update his mental software. He can learn to change old ways and re-program himself in a new and positive way. A computer will give immediate improvements when its software is upgraded. Positive thinking is a powerful way to bring about a change of mind. Coaching is holistic because it deals with every aspect of the client's life and environment.

Each person has a computer brain that works 24 hours a day and is always available. His thoughts and actions are stored in a memory bank. This works rather like software programs that keep a record of all the events of his life. Every thought and every feeling he ever had is registered and can be retrieved on demand. How he makes decisions is recorded. All his hopes and fears and dreams are programmed into the computer brain and given the right commands it can access any intellectual, physical, emotional, social and spiritual information. It works like a software package and like any software package it needs constant updating to keep abreast of new developments.

On my personal computer I have a number of different software packages including word processing, a spreadsheet, a database, art programs and other packages that I have never even tried to use. The only program that I am competent at using is word-processing. I limit the potential of the computer because I have not challenged myself to put in the effort to learn to use all the programs.

Almost every client I meet uses his brain like I use my computer. They use just a tiny part of the talent and intellect they have available to them in their computer brain. They learn to do something well and they know that this is what they are good at doing. It doesn't matter whether it is selling, designing, managing, or problem-solving. They recognise their competence in a given area and they believe that this is it. They are unable to change their thinking because they have never been challenged to update their mental software.

When they come to coaching they rationalise and make excuses for why they are not achieving their potential. They come to their first session of coaching and when I ask 'What stops you from achieving your dream?' they give valid reasons from their way of thinking. They claim to have a lack of education, no talent, been unlucky, lack confidence or their astrological sign is in the wrong orbit. They limit themselves with wrong beliefs.

CONFIDENCE IN THE CLIENT

A Life Coach understands that the software in the computer brain is limited by mental attitudes that need to be challenged. While it is true that some people are smarter and more resourceful than others it is equally true that if one person can do something, anyone else can learn to do it well provided they put in the effort.

One of the most exciting things about coaching is the confidence that the coach shows in the client. Her expectation is that he will set goals that are realistic and achievable. Not everyone with the desire to be a gymnast can be a world-class performer but everyone can reach his or her potential.

The power of coaching is in the mentoring relationship. Think about what you could achieve if you worked with someone who is 100% committed to you and believes that you can and will achieve success. When a person believes in you she models ways for you to believe in yourself. Self-belief is the motivation that powers success.

A Life Coach is dedicated to helping the client improve every area of his life. Some do this so successfully that the client experiences an immediate change. It's one reason why people like international author Anthony Robbins are paid $3000 and more for a single session.

Coaching is a co-operative relationship. The belief of the coach in the willingness of the client to change is in itself a powerful catalyst for change. Robbins's reputation for being successful and getting results is legendary. The key to his success is that he only worked with clients who had already proved that they were willing to change.

One reason why people find it hard to have an accurate understanding of what coaching does for the client is that there are no formulae. Every client is different. Methods that will work with one client will not be useful with another. Some clients are passives and slow to get started. Others are ambitious and nothing will stop them achieving their goals.

Often the client who is dissatisfied with some area of his life is seeking change but he lacks clarity. Even though he says he wants something better he can't name what specifically he is seeking. Many clients who come for coaching say they long for change.

They report that they were given many opportunities to change and they didn't take them or they did but they were unhappy with the outcome.

So many people who come for coaching struggle in life. Some don't want to leave their comfort zones. They know they have gifts and talents that they are not using. A small number recognise that they are scared of success. The fear of change, of giving up the familiar to plunge into the unknown, is too much of a risk for them. They are so paralysed by anxiety and insecurity that they miss many opportunities.

This reminds me of the executive who was at a conference. As he was checking into his hotel he noticed a sign at the reception desk written in large letters. THERE ARE NO PROBLEMS, ONLY OPPORTUNITIES. He later approached the receptionist and said, 'I have a problem.'

The receptionist said with a smile, 'We have no problems here sir, only opportunities.' 'Call it whatever you want,' he said. 'There's a woman in the room that was booked for me.'

It's surprising how many successful clients feel personally unfulfilled. They feel life is passing them by. Almost every client is dissatisfied and dealing with negative feelings that are so familiar that their origins are hard to recognise. They find life hard for whatever reason. Most don't want therapy because they are not into this 'Touchy feely' stuff. They want a practical solution and preferably a quick one.

You cannot deal with a problem until you acknowledge that you have one. The benefit of working with a Life Coach is that she will challenge you to become aware of how you think. Many clients are astonished to discover that they are partly responsible for their own difficulties. They may be obliging people who unconsciously train others to depend on them.

Some people are so N I C E that they allow others to take advantage of their goodness. Colleagues assume that Mr Nice won't mind staying on. 'He's always ready to help out, or whatever.' Mr Nice is rarely aware of how he contributes to his own misery. His coach will question behaviour that trains others to take his co-operation for granted.

A vitally important aspect of one-to-one coaching is the relationship the coach builds with the client. She is a professional mentor who is focused on helping the client in whatever way is necessary. Often simply helping him change his attitude to life and become self-aware brings radical changes rapidly. It is incredibly difficult to give up the old familiar ways of looking at life and move out of your comfort zones to think in a positive way.

Growing in self-awareness will help each client to take responsibility for his actions. When a client understands his role in allowing others to treat him with disrespect he has an insight that will motivate him to act in a healthier way for him. One of the most powerful tools in unlocking the client's potential is to work on self-esteem.

There is a big difference between building self-esteem and flattering a client. The client is his own most important resource. Wherever he goes, whatever he does, he carries himself with him. The sad thing is that most people are unaware of how they self-sabotage with negative self-talk and prevent the success they say they want.

Clients find the instant impact of enhancing self-esteem hard to believe. Therapist Virginia Satir said, 'A very important fact about enhancing self-esteem is that we don't have to grow another leg, change our colour, get a million dollars, be a different age or sex, or get different parents. We need only to change our attitudes and learn new skills. It can happen to everyone.'

SELF-HELP

Coaching is for everyone who wants to be more successful in one
or more areas of his life. There is a myth that Life Coaching is
only for executives and high-flyers. This is because a small
number of high profile internationally known Coaches charge
enormous fees that only the top management in highly successful
companies can afford.

I wrote this book because I am convinced of the benefits of
coaching for everyone. Some talented people need support to
motivate and encourage them to get out of a rut. I have been
meeting people over the past 10 years who are going to
counsellors and healers and diviners because they feel stuck.
They buy every new self-help book that comes on the market and
many admit that they don't even get around to reading these
books.

They attend workshops to meet like-minded people and enjoy the
input but they never seem to make the move they know is
needed. Some love to read about what they should be doing but
fail to follow through on the exercises or advice. They then
blame themselves for not having enough motivation or being lazy
or some other inadequacy on their part.

There are thousands of people who live in a constant state of
dissatisfaction aware that they want to change and unable to
understand why they can't. This book will give them insights
into why they cannot follow through or change despite years of
wanting to help themselves. There is always a positive reason.
Finding out what it is is the key to successful change.

There is no denying that coaching is popular because it works. It
helps people who feel stuck to move forward. Nearly all my
clients come to me through workshops I facilitate or personal

recommendations. Often it is because they see a noticeable difference in a family member or colleague after only a few coaching sessions.

The coach encourages and motivates the client to think in a positive way and the difference this makes is amazing. One reason why Life Coaching offers such quick results is that the majority of newly qualified coaches in Ireland are highly motivated self-starters who bring a variety of skills to this new profession.

The backgrounds of the participants who trained with me as Life Coaches were a banker, an accountant, an award winning counsellor, a medical doctor, a university professor, teachers, civil servants, secretaries and business people. My own background was more varied. I worked as an Educator, Trainer, Writer, Counsellor, Motivational Speaker and NLP Practitioner.

Our varied backgrounds equipped us with different skills and life experiences. Our professional skills will influence how we practice. We are all trained to work with the agenda of any client. There are guidelines for how a coach will work with clients but there is no one formula for success. This is another reason why there is so much confusion about the whole business.

When two people who work with the same coach compare notes they discover that they have totally different experiences. The explanation is simple. They came with different agendas and the coach encouraged each client to use whatever skills he had. She got each client to move forward in the best way for him.

Don't be put off by the terms used in advertising coaching. They are full of jargon. In many of the brochures 'A participative relationship that supports the agenda of the client' is promised. This sounds professional, doesn't it? and it may be off-putting.

The agenda that the client brings is explored and usually it is modified and altered as he becomes clearer about what he really wants.

People come to coaching for many reasons. They recognise that they need help with some difficulty that they cannot resolve themselves. It may seem like a rather minor difficulty to others but for the client it is a problem that creates stress and needs to be addressed. A lack of supportive understanding can make troublesome issues seem unmanageable. Feeling there is no way out and having to put up with a problem has huge repercussions on stress levels.

Clients want results quickly. Some want to be more successful. Others have achieved success but feel there is something missing in their lives. They want something more and are not sure what they are seeking. Others still have job, family or relationship difficulties. Everything from working too hard, failing to get promotion, lack of exercise, health issues or not having a partner are addressed in the sessions with a Life Coach.

High achievers come because they have some symptom that points the finger at a wider discontent and lack of satisfaction in their lives. Common presenting problems are overworking, poor time management, feeling depressed and dissatisfied, procrastination, issues with weight, lacking persistence in the pursuit of goals, not dealing constructively with criticism, wanting to change jobs or find a partner.

When a person is aware that he is stressed out and living with tension he knows there is something amiss. He may tell himself 'I shouldn't feel like this' but his reality is that he feels unfulfilled. When a person has achieved success in his profession and has all the trappings that go with that success and is stressed he often adds to his distress by feeling guilty about feeling miserable or empty.

The presenting issue the client brings is very important to him but it is usually only a symptom of a deeper issue. Let me stress that coaching is not therapy or counselling. The Life Coach who does not have a background in psychology is not qualified to deal with serious psychological problems like clinical depression, addictions or anger management. Once these are excluded almost any other issue you can think of is appropriate.

Among the benefits of working with a coach are;

- You learn about a useful set of tools, systems and practical guidelines for setting goals;
- You have the support and encouragement of a coach who believes in your ability to succeed.
- When you monitor your performance you will value the effort you put in as well as the results.
- You will help yourself to succeed by setting realistic goals that are measurable and achievable.

Change, even change for the good, always brings side effects that have to be carefully examined. The invention of the automobile brought speed and atmospheric pollution. Modern transport gets us there faster and we pay with flabby bodies. In coaching you learn that there is no gain without pain. Change, even change for the better has a cost.

For example a woman is promoted and all her new colleagues are male. She finds it difficult to adjust to a male working environment. She misses networking with her female colleagues. She loses emotional support when she gains promotion. She feels out of her depth but acts as if she is in full control. She comes to her coach for support and to find ways to establish herself in a different environment. She checks out how she might implement new ideas and develop effective relationships with her new colleagues.

Working with a coach she will be helped to identify her strengths and weaknesses. The power of the coaching relationship is that she will get the encouragement that will motivate her to devise coping strategies. She thinks of her investment in coaching as a wise career move that keeps her on track.

Usually if you feel dissatisfied it is because you have a belief that creates the upset. In simple words you want something that you don't have. It may be something you see other people have and you desire. People seek fame, success, a career, money, a partner or whatever they believe will make for happiness.

Many clients who come to coaching think like this. If only they could get whatever they believe makes others happy they would be happy too. Their life would be so different. A smaller number seek support during a time of transition. The coach will assist each client to discover his own resources. How will she do this? By becoming a mentor who mirrors the belief that he can succeed. He will achieve the outcome he desires when he wants it enough or when he learns that it is already within his grasp.

A frog lived all his life in a well. One day he met another frog there.

'Where have you come from?' he asked.

'From the ocean where I live,' said the other.

'What's the ocean like? Is it as big as my well?'

The frog laughed. 'There's no comparison,' he said. 'It's millions of times bigger. You can come and see for yourself.'

The well frog pretended to believe what his visitor said about his ocean home as he politely refused. But he thought, 'Of all the liars I ever met, this one is undoubtedly the biggest and most shameless.'

SUMMARY

- Coaching is a holistic process.
- Change your mind by changing your thinking.
- Learn new skills to enhance self-esteem.
- Coaching is popular because it works.

'Life can only be understood backwards. It must be lived forwards'.

SOREN KIERKEGAARD.

CHAPTER 3

WHAT WILL A COACH DO FOR YOU?

IN THIS CHAPTER:

- **Focus is on the client.**
- **Self-understanding.**
- **The process is important.**
- **Don't take success for granted.**
- **Think in a positive, holistic way.**

'Our deepest fear is not that we are inadequate.
Our deepest fear is that we are powerful beyond measure.'
Nelson Mandela's inaugural speech.

CLIENT FOCUS

The total focus in the coaching relationship is based on the client. The coach works with him in a co-operative relationship so that he will achieve a specific outcome. The presenting issues he brings to the session are addressed. From day one he is encouraged to become aware that the presenting issues do not occur in isolation. If he feels unfulfilled or overworked those feelings have an effect on other aspects of his life.

The coach acts in a supportive, encouraging and challengingly honest manner. Her role is not to eliminate problems but to focus the client on finding within himself resources and strengths that he may not have previously recognised. Once he recognises how resourceful he really is, he can grow in the confidence that he has all the answers.

The coaching relationship is unique in that it offers an extraordinary level of support for the client that is found in no other working relationship. He is helped to become motivated and self-aware. He is invited to pay attention to how he makes meaning of his experiences. In order to make realistic decisions regarding his short-term and longer-term goals he needs to understand himself and his motivation for what he does and how he does it.

You know that Life Coaches have a variety of backgrounds and use different techniques to assist, support and encourage clients to find their own answers. Once the client is really clear about what he wants he will be motivated to introduce and sustain positive behavioural changes in his life that will lead to a more satisfying way of thinking about his life.

The coach deals with the whole person. Results are so quick because she is confident that the client has the answers. She helps him to access what he already knows. Once he understands that his response in any situation is influenced by his way of thinking he has new options. He can change his mind and learn to be happy with whatever happens, like the Park Ranger in the story.

Jogger: 'What kind of weather are we going to have today?'
Park Ranger: 'The kind of weather I like.'
Jogger: 'How do you know it will be the kind of weather you like?'
Park Ranger: 'Having found out, sir, that I cannot always get what I like, I have learned to like what I get. So I am quite sure we will have the kind of weather I like.'

IS IT ABOUT GOALS?

There is a widespread perception that coaching is only about goal-setting. Achieving goals is important but even more important is the process. The steps that need to be taken on the way to achieving a positive outcome for the client involve complex decisions that take account of a whole range of issues that few people consider.

The preliminary goals that a person brings to coaching are usually changed and modified many times before the ultimate goal is set. Goal setting is only part of an ongoing process that involves personal and professional development. Coaches with a background in NLP understand how people think and communicate. These are invaluable tools for helping the client to understand that his response to what he believes is true dictates his behaviour. As Henry Ford said, 'Whether you believe you can or you can't do something, you are right.'

The coach supports and guides the client in setting up a structured programme that is broken down into the various steps that need to be attended to on the way to achieving the outcomes he wants. Usually there will be a specific timeframe agreed for each action on the way to the goal. One result of breaking or chunking a task down is that the client will experience a sense of success with each completed step. People with a tendency to procrastinate have a sense of being overwhelmed by tasks that become manageable when broken down into different components.

Self-motivators who organise and plan well also benefit from such programmes. They often take success for granted and fail to acknowledge their own efforts. Colleagues pick up on this 'Success is taken for granted' approach and when the task is successfully completed avoid giving them the recognition that they give to others. I need hardly explain that if colleagues who look for plaudits are lauded for lesser achievements, the self-motivator's successful outcome is overshadowed.

People who have expectations of success, take it for granted, and move on to the next task are not putting a value on their achievements. Many professionally successful people do not know how they feel. One result of this lack of awareness is that they miss out on the good feelings and fun of achievement that gives meaning and value to their efforts.

PERCEPTIONS

Nobody really knows how anybody else thinks. We each perceive the world in which we live in a unique and subjective way. We have our own attitudes, beliefs and values and these have an impact on how we respond to life experiences. When a coach invites a client to say how he feels about completing the steps on the way to achieving his goals she invites the client to become aware of the 'Feel-good factor' that everyone needs, but may not acknowledge that they need.

The coach co-operates with the client as he designs and sets up a structured plan. She will challenge him to find his inner resources in order to build his confidence and deal with personal issues. He is the one who will do the work to achieve each step on the way to his goals. She holds him accountable for staying on track. Many clients who appear to be very successful in their chosen careers have incredibly low self-esteem. When they improve their self-esteem they also improve their self-confidence and this improvement changes their perceptions of how they are doing.

WHAT COACHING IS NOT

Life Coaching can trace its heritage back to mentoring programmes and executive coaching in large organisations. This is how the myth that it is only for high-flyers and executives was spawned. The models that come from management and organisational development are useful in training situations.

They are different from the model of Sports Coaching that is familiar to so many people. It is true that in some organisations the manager is expected to act like a Sports Coach, provide a game plan and work with a team to increase productivity and profits. These associations with coaching in large organisations and Sports Coaching are less than helpful.

Some of the methods that are used in fitness training and on the sports field give Life Coaching a bad name. Many of the Trainers and Coaches who work with internationally recognised football teams or individual sports stars are very successful. It is widely recognised that these coaches play an important role in the successful outcome the teams or individuals achieve.

Their methods for achieving success may involve putting the client under extreme duress and pressure. There is no denying that the Sports Coach works hard to train, motivate and support the sports star or players. At every step on the way towards achieving the successful outcome the coach is there, believing in the individual or team, supporting and encouraging each person to believe that he can succeed and that he has all the resources he needs to achieve success.

The role of a Sports Coach is to support, cajole, pressurise and push a person to his limits. Television pictures of driven trainers and coaches who shout and scream as they push clients to go beyond their limits of endurance in order to achieve the success of a peak performance are distressing to watch.

In the sports forum some coaches work to get their clients to the peak of success by using endurance training that is both painful and harsh. The methods used to help athletes achieve success in Sports Coaching bear no resemblance to the respectful and co-operative relationship in Life Coaching that is the key to unlocking the client's potential and achieving his goals.

Other models of coaching that people are familiar with are the niche coaches who have a very specific expertise, for example; the Speech Coach; Sales Coach; Drama Coach or Personal Fitness Coach. The Life Coach is not subject focused. She is person focused and can work equally successfully with the agenda of any client. Coaches work with people at every level. Executives, managers, sales representatives, homemakers, doctors, teachers and unemployed people all benefit from Life Coaching.

POSITIVE FOCUS

A popular definition of coaching is 'The art of facilitating the performance, learning and development of another.' One way the coach encourages the client to achieve personal success is by learning how to become self-aware and to think in a more positive and holistic way. It's hard to believe that many outwardly successful people have very poor self-esteem and lack self-worth.

It's amazing how self-confidence is boosted in a client who learns to stop putting himself down. In this book you will learn how important it is to listen to your own self-talk and keep it positive. For now it is enough to say that when negative thinking is challenged and reframed into more positive thinking immediate changes occur. Positive thinking creates positive feelings.

Many people who are dealing with issues and problems think in a negative way. They are masters at blaming. Some have very 'Black and white' thinking with no exploration of the middle ground. They know what they don't want but find it hard to say what they really like or want. Like the guy who dolefully opened his lunchbox. 'Oh no,' he said aloud. 'Cheese sandwiches again!' This happened a second and a third and a fourth day. Then a co-worker who had heard the mutterings of the man said, 'If you hate cheese sandwiches so much why don't you get your wife to make you some other type?' 'Because I'm not married. I make those sandwiches myself.'

Many clients in coaching find it very helpful when they learn to reframe. Take a statement like 'I don't want to procrastinate.' To reframe simply ask yourself this question. 'When I don't want to procrastinate what is it that I do want?' If there is a negative in that answer go one step further.

Say the reply is 'I don't want to miss deadlines.' Ask, 'If I succeed in not missing deadlines what do I want?' The negative is now changed to a more positive answer, 'I want to meet my deadlines.' That change is subtle. It gives the client a sense that he has control. Saying 'I want' creates a sense of being in charge of the choices he makes. Altering one word may not appear to be a big deal but that tiny change makes the difference that makes the difference.

With the help of the coach the client can discover that language is a positive tool that can be used to change perception and build self-esteem. Once he learns how to listen to himself he will recognise when he speaks in negative ways. He can learn to reframe in a positive way. This will focus him on positive thinking and help him have a clearer outcome. It's beautiful to see the immediate change that more positive thinking makes. He will be more motivated to discover what steps he needs to take in order to get the positive results he wants.

Positive reframing, deciding on the outcome you want, is more complicated than most people imagine because change does not occur in isolation. Do something different in one area of your life and you will find that will bring about changes in other areas.

Don't take my word for this. Experience what happens. Please do the following exercise. Changing a negative way of thinking and reframing in a positive way is the first step to achieving a healthy outcome for you.

EXERCISE ON POSITIVE REFRAMING

Write a list of five things you don't want to do.

_____

_____

_____

_____

_____

Go back to each item on the list. Ask yourself 'When I don't want to do_____, what is it I do want? Keep asking the question and writing the answers until you have a list of five positive things that you do want.

_____

_____

_____

_____

_____

_____

_____

_____

Write the reframed list of five positive things you now want.

_____

_____

_____

_____

_____

_____

_____

_____

_____

_____

HOW CAN YOU GET THIS AND WHEN DO YOU WANT IT?

1 _____

2 _____

3 _____

4 _____

5 _____

WHAT COULD STOP YOU?

_____

_____

_____

_____

_____

Don't be tempted to skip this exercise. You may think you don't need to write down that list of five things you don't want to do but trust me. This exercise is useful because it challenges you to think. This brings interesting insights that will prove surprisingly helpful. Some people find that they already have many of the things on their list already. Or with very little effort they could have some of them.

It only takes seconds to make a list of five things that a person knows that they don't want. It takes a little longer to explore how it is possible to turn negative statements around and make them positive. It takes time and commitment to be specific and to put a time-frame on when you want things.

Imagine I am doing this exercise and this is the list of things that I don't want to do.

I don't want;

- to be late.
- to make the dinner.
- to have a late night.
- to put on weight.
- to write the report my boss wants on Monday.

The second step is to go back over each item and ask 'When I don't want to be late what it is that I do want?' That looks easy to reframe in a positive way. 'I don't want to be late' can be reframed positively as 'I want to be on time.' So I can fill that in.

My second statement is more difficult. When I say 'I don't want to make the dinner.' I know what I don't want to do but I have to eat. I need to think about what it is I really want. I need food to keep me alive so I have very little choice about eating. I could skip dinner once or twice but that is not a practical solution in the longer term. The issue here is not the dinner, it's the making of the meal.

FINDING THE ISSUE

So I need time to identify what's going on for me. Maybe I feel tired today and it's only today that I don't want to make dinner. When it is a specific and not an ongoing issue it becomes easy to reframe, 'I don't want to make dinner today. I want to have dinner cooked and served to me.' Once I am clear about the location where I want this to happen I have found my own solution. This is a satisfactory reframe.

For the person who never wants to make dinner it is difficult to come up with a reframe. Until he is clear and has worked out a solution, how can he be positive about what he wants? Once you are clear about what you want the next step is to ask, 'How do you get what you want?' This is where the coaching relationship comes into its own. The coach will hold the client accountable. She wants what is best for each client's overall wellbeing.

Filling in an exercise sheet is one way to think about your options but it does not challenge you to move forward. A coach will encourage you to move out of your comfort zone and think in more creative ways. A person who wants to eat and is not prepared to make dinner has reasons that make sense to him. When the consequences of how he reframes are challenged by a coach he will usually find options that he would never have dreamed of on his own.

A coach will follow through on every suggestion the client offers. He is encouraged to reflect on the consequences of each decision he contemplates. Often what will work very well in the short term will be found to be inappropriate in the longer term.

UNDERSTANDING CHOICES

Let's fantasise that a guy who lives on his own doesn't want to cook. He brainstorms and comes up with the following list of positive options.

- I could eat cooked meals from the supermarket.
- I could order in and have food delivered to my home.
- I could go to a restaurant to eat.
- I could get sandwiches from the shop.
- I could get fast food from a drive-through.
- I could hire a chef.

He could do all of these in the short term. They may even appear practical when he comes up with them first. A self-help book cannot challenge these answers in the way a real live person could. Reading 'Do you want to do this EVERY DAY?' will not have the same impact as facing a coach whose facial expressions and tone of voice will challenge the client to explore the consequences further. Working with a non-judgemental mentor who is focused on encouraging the client to be the best he can be creates a powerful motivation. The focus in coaching is to ensure that the decisions the client makes are appropriate to his lifestyle and good health.

The solution that may be expedient and helpful for one client may be totally inappropriate for another who has different issues to be addressed. So you can see that there is no problem in reframing some issues like 'I don't want to have a late night.' A change to 'I want an early night' is obvious. Others like 'I don't want to put on weight' are harder to reframe because the client needs to learn about the impact of using negatives like 'don't' as well as stating in a positive way what he really wants.

In order to set any goal one must discover what motivates a person to do or not do certain things. The final issue, 'I don't want to write the report my boss wants on Monday' is another complex issue that is hard to reframe. By now you understand that what seems like a very simple exercise has great potential to reveal how you think and feel.

Positive reframing exercises are useful for discovering what you think and why you think in that way. These exercises also challenge you to become self-aware. When you discover that many of the things you say you want can be yours with very little effort it raises another question. Why have you failed to get what you think you want? Always you will find that there is a good reason. You may like to have it but are not prepared to make the effort that is required to get it.

The final item on the list is the report for Monday. My reluctance to write a report is the presenting issue. When I check in with what my beliefs are about this I find that it is only part of a problem that includes feelings about the work involved in putting the report together, the desire to do other things and awareness of the consequences if the report is late. It could also involve the inability to get motivated or prioritise or the desire to concentrate on other work.

That answer to a question like, 'When you don't want to write the report what is it that you want to do?' is the beginning of growing in the self-awareness that is necessary for ongoing positive reframing. When I keep repeating the question I eventually get to the real outcome I want. Let's go through a fairly typical list.

I don't want to write the report my boss wants on Monday.

- When I don't want to write the report what is it I want?
- I don't want him finding fault with my work.
- When I don't want him finding fault with my work what is it I want?
- I don't want him giving out.

- When I don't want him giving out what is it I want?
- I don't want hassle.
- When I don't want to hassle what is it I want?
- I want him to say exactly what way he wants me to lay out the report.
- I want him to appreciate the work involved.
- I want my work to be valued.

Once you are clear in your own mind about what you want you are ready to ask 'What stops me from getting it?' To change what you do not like it is helpful to know what you really like and want. If you have a complaint it's useful to offer suggestions as to how that complaint can be put right.

It's amazing that many clients are unwilling to ask for what they want. They feel shy or inhibited and 'The Gremlin' voice issues warnings of dire happenings. So they seethe with resentment and blame others for personal distress that they are co-responsible for creating.

SUMMARY

- **Learn to reframe.**
- **Discover what you want.**
- **When do you want it?**
- **What are the consequences of getting what you want?**

'To live a single day and hear a good teaching is better than to live a hundred years without knowing such teaching'.

Buddha (B.C. 568-488).

CHAPTER 4

WHEEL OF LIFE

IN THIS CHAPTER:

- **Overview - find what is working.**
- **You can always find something good in a situation.**
- **Your life experience is yours.**
- **What gives your life meaning?**
- **Think in a new way.**

A young composer once came to consult Mozart on how to develop his talent.
'I would advise you to start with simple things,' Mozart said. 'Songs for example.'
'But you were composing symphonies when you were a child,' the man protested.
'True enough,' said Mozart. 'But I didn't have to go to anyone for advice on how to develop my talent.'

ENLIGHTENED SELF-INTEREST

A farmer whose corn always took first prize at the County Fair had the habit of sharing his best grain seeds with all the farmers in his neighbourhood. Many of his neighbours thought he was crazy.

When asked why he was so generous he said, 'It is really a matter of enlightened self-interest. The wind picks up the pollen and carries it from field to field. So if my neighbours grow inferior grains the cross pollination brings down the quality of my crop. That is why I want them to have the best seeds. Then they plant only the best. They get good seeds and are happy. I get prize-winning crops and I am happy too.'

COACHING THE WHOLE PERSON

The first or intake session is fascinating for a Life Coach because each client brings his own agenda. He has a unique approach to life. Some clients are very clear about what they want. Others are aware that something needs to change but seek help to find out what specifically that is.

The coach will take note of every issue the client brings to the first coaching session. She will also be sensitive to issues that the client may not yet be aware of and that he needs to work on. Underneath the presenting issue that almost every client brings to coaching there is always a lack of fulfilment.

Many clients enjoy the external trappings of success but they are dissatisfied. They know they want something more but they cannot say what it is they want or lack. The coach recognises that lack is rooted in the human need to have a purpose and meaning in life. The client is seeking fulfilment.

There is great emphasis placed today on holistic living. Many people dismiss the talk of wholeness and being aware of the mind/body/spirit connection as just a passing fad. They are willing to accept that the human person is not just physical but has an emotional aspect. Some are unaware that they have genuine spiritual needs too.

Effective Life Coaches encourage the client to begin with an overview of where he is currently at, how he got there and where he wants to go. If he is dissatisfied with life when he is outwardly successful he can be certain that his life is out of balance. He recognises that something is not right. Usually he will discover that he is neglecting to take care of needs he is not aware he has.

When any one area in the client's life is neglected or ignored it has an impact on every other area. Some people have been brainwashed into needing approval. They bury themselves in their work and neglect their social life. They enjoy professional success and get the approval they need but they miss out on having fun.

Others are programmed to put the needs of others first. They wear themselves out caring, fail to meet their own needs and end up resenting others for taking advantage. Others still work hard and play hard. They don't give themselves any time for rest or reflection. They live in a state of overdrive always on the go and rarely take time to assess the quality of their lives. When any one area is neglected it has an impact on the person's overall happiness.

YOU ARE RESOURCEFUL

As a coach I believe the client has all the resources he needs to meet the full agenda that he brings. He just doesn't recognise them yet. Most clients like to be told, 'You have all the answers.' Some don't believe this. It's my job to reassure each client that 'If you don't yet have them you can and will find the answers.'

Clients are often pleasantly surprised to find that coaching creates a context for them to work on personal issues that they previously ignored or failed to see as relevant. The presenting issues are always important because the client is focused on dealing with these immediately. His expectations are that he will successfully manage the agenda he brings.

To achieve any goal involves the hard work of self-awareness. Having professional qualifications and skills are only the beginning. They are the external aspects but the internal responses are the key to success or failure. Later you will be invited to work on a well-formed outcome, to look at your values and beliefs, to identify the life strategies you use before exploring your goals.

Usually a client will find that in this process his aspirations expand. When you become more self-aware you will begin to take better care of yourself. When one aspect of your life improves it has a knock-on effect and improves every other area. Clients find that when they bring more balance into how they live their vision broadens and they achieve way beyond their initial narrow goals.

The coach sets out to work with a client to encourage him to set goals that reflect his values and life purpose. It is a process that is led by the client. She invites him to draw the map for his journey. She has travelled with many clients and can make suggestions about the territory. The result of this co-active relationship is that the client finds insights and has experiences of self-discovery that are life-changing.

The fundamental nature of a co-active coaching relationship is that the coach and client are active collaborators. The coach recognises that the client is creative and resourceful. The agenda comes from the client. The relationship is an alliance between two equals for the purpose of meeting the client's needs. Co-active coaching addresses the client's whole life.

I use the 'Wheel of Life Exercise' at my intake sessions because it is a powerful tool for taking an inventory. It serves as a baseline and guideline. When you have completed the exercise you will understand what you like about your life and what you're not happy about and want to change.

You will have insights that help you understand yourself better. As a Life Coach I take an integrated approach that takes account of the whole person. The intake session in one-to-one coaching is a wonderful experience that most clients experience as very encouraging.

To have the experience of feeling unconditionally accepted is rare. To have a willing mentor who challenges you to see that you have unconsciously created a belief system for yourself that motivates everything you do and say is pleasant. To have someone who believes that you had positive reasons for everything you ever did, even when the results were disastrous, is exceptional.

In the exercise on positive reframing you learned how to be clear about what you do and don't want to do. Adapt the exercise to work out what you like and don't like. When you reflect on your answers you can sub-divide those categories into what you would like and don't have or have and don't like or don't have and would not want to have. For example you might like to have a holiday home in Spain or be promoted but don't see any great prospects of getting them. That's what you would like and don't have. The 'Have and don't like' might be a jealous spouse or an addiction to cigarettes or poor self-esteem.

It's fascinating to see the reaction when I ask a client 'What don't you have and don't want to have.' The initial puzzlement gives way to understanding when I explain. 'Some people list things like a broken marriage, a life challenging illness like cancer, bankruptcy.' Most people feel a sense of gratitude after this exercise.

For many people it is a totally new experience to have someone listen in a non-judgemental way and accept that he has always had a good reason for everything he did and did not do. This does not mean that the coach will condone inappropriate actions. She will separate the action from the person and his motivation. This acceptance invites the client to acknowledge his responsibility. She will ask curious questions that challenge new thinking.

In coaching 'Failure' is redefined and looked at as an opportunity to learn from the consequences. Examining what worked is important. Finding out what didn't work and why is vital.

INTAKE SESSION

I'm trained to see the positive strengths in a client even when he fails to see them himself. If I were with you now I would want you to know that I see a complex person with many different aspects to his life who is motivated to make the changes he desires.

You have dreams and aspirations and passions for your life that you may never have shared with anyone before. Underneath whatever your presenting reasons are for coming to coaching you want change. You no longer want things in your life to continue as they are now and I have every confidence in your motivation to achieve what is right for you beginning today.

So let's begin work. Before you go any further I want you to get yourself one of those plastic envelope type folders. You probably know the ones I mean. You can keep this book and your paper and pens safely in them because they close with a stud fastener and the contents won't fall out.

You will need;

- Pens;
- 3 different coloured markers;

- a small pocketsize notebook;

- a ruler

- paper clips;

- loose-leaved paper or a jotter from which you can tear pages easily.

I want you to do an exercise to assess your life and see if it is in balance. I want you to be honest with yourself as you explore each important area. When you know that you can change what you want to change you also need to know that each change will have an impact on other areas of your life.

Let me explain something that is important for you to know. You will find that you can meet your goals if you are prepared to put in the work and effort consistently but don't be surprised if you find that the price is too high. When you take an overview and see the full picture you may discover that you want to rethink your goals. If that's what you decide that is okay too.

This intake exercise will help you find out what you like about your life, what is working well and what you want to reassess. In the process you will have insights that will help you discover your life's passion, re-examine your deepest values and beliefs, expand your thinking about your desired outcome and find direction.

LIFE INVENTORY

You don't live your life in discrete compartments. There are many different aspects to your life and you want to see how you are doing in each area. In the exercise section at the back of the book you will find a blank wheel. If the headings that I suggest you use don't suit your circumstances feel free to change them and use what works for you.

1. Work and career.
2. Family.
3. Social Life.
4. Money.
5. Fun and recreation.
6. Self-care.
7. Health.
8. Spirituality.

This exercise will help you to make an inventory for each part of your life and rank your level of satisfaction. I'm not sure if you are familiar with the concept of having different parts or aspects to your life. Let me explain.

Have you ever found yourself pulled in two directions at the one time? One part of you wants something. Another part of you doesn't want it. You have a problem making up your mind and the tension between what you do and don't want to do stresses you out. A common situation that will illustrate what I mean has to do with food.

Have you ever had the situation where one part of you wants a second slice of that luscious chocolate cake? Another part of you is counting calories. A little voice in your head is arguing with itself.
'Ah go on, you may as well be nice to yourself.'
'That cake is a calorie bomb. You really don't need it, you've already had some.'
'It was delicious. I want some more.'
'If you take another slice you'll put on weight.'

You can see how the struggle to decide on something as unimportant as eating an extra slice of cake has an effect on your stress levels. There are many different aspects to your life and when any one area is out of alignment with the others your life is out of balance.

I have listed eight areas in the following exercise.

1. Work and career.
2. Family.
3. Social Life.
4. Money.
5. Fun and Recreation.
6. Self-care.
7. Health.
8. Spirituality.

The wheel is a symbol for balance. If your life is not in balance you will need to do something that will bring your life into balance, won't you? All of these different parts are linked and a change in one area will affect every other area.

WHEEL OF LIFE EXERCISE

Take a pen and put a mark on the line corresponding to the numbered areas on the headings. 0 at the centre shows zero satisfaction and 10 on the outer rim indicates the maximum level of satisfaction.

Create a new outer image by connecting the marks you made and you have a graphic illustration of whether life is giving you a smooth or bumpy ride.

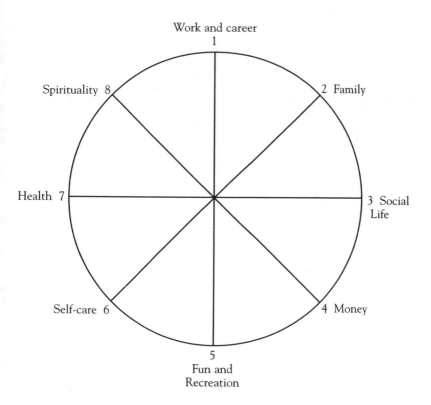

If your get a result like this, your wheel is out of alignment. Your life is out of balance. How bumpy would the ride be if this were a real wheel?

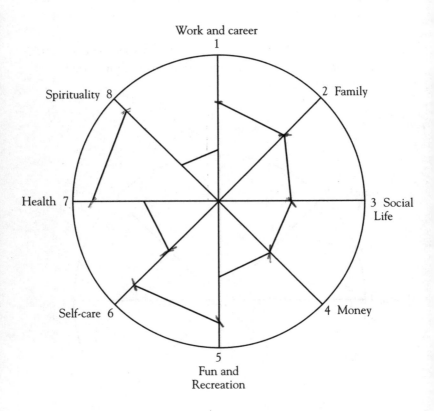

As I can't see your finished 'Wheel of Life' I will invite you to do the following exercise. Let's begin this life inventory by exploring what is working well in each area.

Write one sentence about five things that are working well under each heading.

Work and career

_____

_____

_____

_____

_____

Family

_____

_____

_____

_____

_____

Social Life

_____

_____

_____

_____

_____

Money

_____

_____

_____

_____

_____

Fun and recreation

_____

_____

_____

_____

_____

Self-care

_____

_____

_____

_____

_____

Health

_____

_____

_____

_____

_____

Spirituality

_____

_____

_____

_____

WORK AND CAREER.

Be really honest with yourself when you say what is working for you. If you enjoy the perks of the job but hate the work write down the perks. We'll come back to the negatives later. No one is going to judge your answers. If you dislike your work and your first instinct is to say 'I hate this job, I can't find anything that is good about it,' I want you to go beyond that and find something that you like.

No matter how bad a situation is there is always something positive you can find. Look for the good even if in the beginning it seems too hard. Use humour. 'I get paid,' or 'I work in a building that shelters me from rain' may be the best you can manage. You will always find something positive if you try hard enough. It's worth the effort because it helps you become aware that you always have multiple choices.

Continue this exercise in the frame of mind that you will find positive things to say about every section.

Family

You are the person you are today because of all of your life experiences. Your family is important. Remember that your relationship with your parents had a powerful impact on your self-confidence and self-esteem. If it's helpful for you, list what you like about your present family and make a sub-heading for what was good in your family of origin.

Social Life

You're not looking for anything dramatic. If you have a wonderful social life, gadding about the world that's great. And if your social life consists of going to the pub with colleagues or having a few friends in for a take-away and a bottle of wine that's what you write down.

Money

Don't underestimate the importance of having or not having financial stability. If you are wealthy and have no financial worries you will find this an easy exercise. If you are financially embarrassed I am challenging you to tune in to what you like about the challenges of impoverished cash flow. Later we will do other exercises that will put you in touch with the negatives and positives of each situation.

Fun and recreation

These are linked and they are different. You may find that the same kinds of answers that you gave to Social Life come up for recreation. Or you may find that your answers are different because your recreational needs involve getting away from people. Either way is acceptable.

How do you have fun? Think back and check if you still enjoy the things you did for fun when you were younger. Even if you haven't done something for several years you can still put it on the list.

Self-care

When you are making an inventory of your life it's vital to pay close attention to how you take care of yourself. What do you like about how you care for your body and your mind and your spirit.

Health

Most people take their health for granted. They rarely stop to appreciate how wonderful it is to be able to see and hear and walk. To stop and think about what is good about your health or to ask 'How healthy am I?' can be a wake up call. When you're fit and healthy you have energy and it is wise to use that well.

Spirituality

Many people believe that if they do not attend church or worship in a community of believers that they are not spiritual. Once you understand that there is a difference between religion and spirituality there is no problem in recognising how important it is to be aware of this aspect of how you live.

A client may not be religious in the denominational sense but he has a spiritual dimension to his life. Understanding who he is and

how he is in the world and what gives meaning to his life is his
spirituality. In that sense everyone in the world has a spiritual
dimension and a purpose for living.

MAKING CONNECTIONS

Every area of your life is interconnected. Say you work longer
hours to gain a promotion. That may put you under stress and
that in turn could affect your health. Your health affects your
energy level, which in turn has an impact on how you feel when
you are with your family.

I don't need to go on. You have got the idea. A change in one
area will have an impact on every other area. Some changes are
major and their consequences are very clear. Most are so minor
that you pay them no attention and have little awareness of how
you are affected by them.

After doing this exercise I'm making an educated guess that you
are telling yourself, 'Well I never thought about it like that before.'
That's good. I want you to begin to think about things in a new
way. You will be pleasantly surprised when you discover how
quickly your feelings change when you learn to create a positive
focus for every area of your life.

I'm not asking you to be unrealistic. I'm not asking you to pretend
that everything in the garden is rosy. You wouldn't need to work
with a coach if they were. What I am encouraging you to do is to
learn that there are many different ways to think about the same
situation. When you think in a positive way your feelings follow
and you will feel more positive. Like the child in a geography
class who was asked what are the benefits of longitude and
latitude. 'You can use them to have you rescued. When you are
drowning you can call out what longitude and latitude you are in
and the lifeguards will know where to find you.'

SUMMARY

- Find what is working.
- You can always find something good in a situation.
- Your life experience is yours.
- What gives your life meaning?
- Think in a new way.

'Every man is his own ancestor, and every man is his own heir. He devises his own future and he inherits his own past'.

FREDERICK HENRY HODGE (1805-1890).

CHAPTER 5

WHY GOALS ARE NECESSARY

IN THIS CHAPTER:

- **Having goals is important.**
- **Behaviour has a structure and meaning.**
- **You have choices about what you think.**
- **Check your motivation.**
- **Goals clarification.**
- **Are all my parts in harmony?**

'What you tell yourself you are you will be.
What you allow yourself to be reflects what you have told
yourself you are'.

Iyanla Vanzant

'Why don't we aim during the next ten years to have peace on earth.
That could be the greatest honour we could bestow upon our
generation. So if we do that, then people will be here two thousand
years from now. People should set goals they can never reach. I'm not
going to rest until all the world's problems have been solved.'

Ted Turner founder of the Goodwill Games,
CNN, TNT and Headline News.

HAVING GOALS IS IMPORTANT

In 1953 in Yale University only 3% of the final year class had
written a life-plan. Twenty years later in 1973 a researcher
checked with the class of '53 and found that the 3% with written

goals had accumulated more wealth than all of the other 97% together. This result was so unexpected that the researchers then looked at relationships, family and work and they discovered that the 3% who had goals were also doing better in every other area of their lives.

I'm not suggesting that you should embark on every little activity with a conscious goal in mind. That would be impractical. What I am suggesting is that you become aware of your own intentions for doing or omitting to do things. People usually act without any conscious intention. They behave in a certain way because they have an unconscious belief that the behaviour will benefit them. I want you to recognise that whether you are aware of it or not your behaviour has a purpose and a meaning.

Coaching builds on this innate need for purpose and meaning that is in every person. The coach encourages the client to pay attention to what he is thinking. This will make him become aware of his own motivation. We all know talented people who never seem to accomplish anything. I have no evidence to say that this is because they don't have goals. However there is a great deal of evidence to show that many very successful people believe their success is due to having clear, measurable goals. They know what they want and they go after it.

There is a very fine line between success and failure. In an earlier chapter you saw how important it is to be clear about what it is you want. One definition of a goal is 'The object of a person's ambition or effort; an aim or desired result.' Your goals are the desired outcomes you want for yourself stated in a positive way.

FLEXIBLE GOALS

Among the benefits of having a Life Coach is the mentoring relationship. The coach will get you to expand your thinking.

She will invite you to think about aspects of your goal that would not occur to you without her intervention. Her questions will get you to consider the tiny details that are relevant to success or failure. Almost everyone who works with a coach comes to recognise that they have strengths and resources they have not recognised or valued. When you feel that you are a resourceful person you develop self-belief.

When another has confidence in your ability to work and be successful in achieving your outcome you are empowered to achieve. In the process of working with a coach the client is encouraged to acknowledge his own strengths and the resources he has that he may not have previously valued.

He will write and rewrite his goals many times. Sometimes he will discover that it is necessary to abandon a goal. On investigation he finds that it is not worth wanting. Understanding for what purpose you want something and asking what will it do for you if you get it is a useful exercise. It challenges you to think of consequences.

Thinking in a positive way does not come easily to some but it is a necessary skill that can be learned. Negative thinking creates a negative outlook, which gives power to negative feelings. It drains your energy and deadens your capacity to enjoy life. Developing the knowledge and skills to set positive goals about ordinary everyday things will energise you, help you to become self-aware and build your self-confidence. Feeling good about yourself and your abilities will equip you for the tasks ahead.

The brain neurology involved in how we perceive things is fascinating. The way you think powerfully affects how you feel. You already understand that you have choices about what you think. You understand why many people, when they are asked about their goals, say what they don't want. They are not clear about their real desires and personal values. Without that clarity they simply can't move forward. In order to set realistic and practical goals, you must be willing to think in a different way.

To understand what it is you don't want your brain has to make a mental representation. Usually this involves some kind of image and the mind uses that mental imagery. If I tell you 'Don't think of a pink elephant' you have to create a mental representation of a pink elephant in order to understand what I asked you not to think about. To understand whether a goal is worth wanting you will need to be clear about what it is you want.

Lack of success always involves lack of clarity. Unclear goals, poor motivation and self-doubt all play a part in failure. 'What do you want?' and 'For what purpose do you want it?' are questions that bring up interesting insights when you are honest with yourself.

MINOR GOAL EXERCISE

Write down 5 goals or outcomes you want without thinking too deeply about them. Be realistic. Make sure they are achievable and written in a positive way. Rewrite if necessary.

No.1 _____

No.2 _____

No.3 _____

No.4 _____

No.5 _____

Write one benefit for each goal.

No.1 _____

No.2 _____

No.3 _____

No.4 _____

No.5 _____

Now explore what stops you from getting that goal or outcome.

No.1 _____

_____

_____

No.2 _____

_____

_____

No.3 _____

_____

_____

No.4 _____

_____

No.5 _____

_____

_____

REALITY CHECK

I'm making an educated guess that you discovered that if you really want to you can have some of the things on your wish list. It's amazing how often people believe they want something but fail to make the effort to get what they want.

At a recent social gathering a woman was talking about taking photographs from a small plane. A 40 years old man told us that he had wanted to be a pilot all his life. Another man in the company mentioned that there was a small airfield near where the first man lived. He told us that his son went there for private flying lessons. The 'Aspiring pilot' didn't know about either the airfield or the availability of flying lessons.

The truth is that much of what we think we want is achievable. Often we allow people and circumstances to dictate what we can and can't do. Or we are simply not prepared to put in the effort. For many people when they really think about what they want they discover that they have worthwhile goals but that they are not motivated to put in the effort to achieve them. Or they have wrong ideas that create negative beliefs about success that stop them and like the aspiring pilot they miss opportunities.

PRELIMINARY GOAL SETTING EXERCISE

For this exercise you will need one pen to write with and two different coloured pens or markers and paper.

Think of a goal you would like to achieve. Don't choose something that is difficult. On a scale of 1-10 with 10 being the ultimate goal, go for about a 4. Make sure you write your goal positively.

_____

_____

Why do you want this goal? Don't pay any attention to spelling or punctuation at this juncture, just write.

When you are finished read over what you have written very carefully. Get two different coloured highlighter pens. Please circle every positive statement in one colour and any negative statements in a different colour.

Now you are going to reframe every negative statement into a positive one. You already know how to do this. Go back to every negative statement that you have circled and answer this question. 'When I tell myself that I don't want (examine the first negative statement) what is it that I do want?'

If that statement is also negative keep asking the question, 'When I tell myself that I don't want (take the first negative statement) what is it that I do want?' Continue to ask this question until you come to a reply that is positive. Do this for each statement that is negative.

Rewrite your goal in one sentence. Briefly say why you want this goal. This is an exercise that will train you to become aware of negative thinking and teach you how to reframe in a positive way.

_____

_____

_____

_____

_____

_____

_____

_____

_____

_____

SETTING GOALS

Now that you have clarity about how to set a positive goal, and understand your reasons for wanting that outcome let's move on. On a scale of one to ten, ten being the major goal go for about a six. You know what to do.

Write your positive goal. In fantasy experience how your life will be different when you have this goal. In other words dream the dream and write about the experience. Describe as vividly as possible what you will see, hear and feel when you achieve the outcome you desire. Use your imagination and create the picture of how you will be when the goal is realised.

My goal is _____

_____

_____

When I achieve that outcome:

I will see _____

_____

I will hear _____

_____

I will feel _____

_____

I will smell, taste or touch _____

_____

_____

What are your positive reasons for wanting this goal?

_____

_____

_____

_____

_____

_____

What will you gain when you get this?

_____

_____

_____

_____

_____

_____

What will you lose of value when you get this?

_____

_____

_____

_____

_____

_____

How will having this make you feel?

_____

_____

_____

_____

_____

_____

CLARIFYING GOALS

Identifying your goals is the easy part of the exercise. Goal clarification, understanding why you want this and exploring the impact on your life of getting it is the hard part. Why? It takes time and hardly anyone realises that when you achieve any goal, no matter how small, something has to change in your life. When you gain wealth you lose poverty. The gains and losses always need to be explored because what appears to be a positive can sometimes turn out to be negative in the longer term. Living in the luxury that is one person's delight can be life destroying for another.

A long time ago a rare bird alighted in a very rich man's palace. The rich man was delighted. He ordered that food from his own table be offered to the bird and that his orchestra be brought to play for its enjoyment.

The other birds envied his good luck. But the bird looked miserable and dazed. It refused to touch any of the unfamiliar food offered to it and, in a short time, it contracted a sickness and died.

The luxury that delighted the rich man destroyed the quality of life and killed the bird.

Coaching helps you recognise that one's desires are far more complex than most of us realise. For example a popular item on many lists is 'I want to win the lottery.' That is a desire that is shared by millions of people but it is not a very realistic goal, is it? The chances of success are very small and outside one's control. Unless Lady Luck smiles sweetly on the person it's a goal he is unlikely to achieve.

WINNING THE LOTTERY

Let's suppose that winning the lottery is your intended goal. It's an outcome millions of people say they want. For that reason it's an interesting example to work with as we are learning to assess and clarify our desired outcome.

Any time you gain an outcome you want, something in your life will also change. You will lose something else. Whether you ever thought about it or not there are wonderful and painful consequences to achieving any goal, even to winning a fortune. Having money may be a change for the better and what you lose is poverty - something you wanted to lose anyway.

You may find that when you fully explore all aspects of what being rich would mean to you that you're not prepared to deal with the impact the change would have on your life. You get new insights, your thinking changes. You see the downside and you may discover that you don't really want what you thought would make you happy. It's amazing to make this discovery, to find that whatever you believed would change your life and make you happy is not worth wanting.

LIFE COACHING

Let's stay with the lottery example, work with an unrealistic goal and see how you can deepen your understanding of how coaching works. If a client has the goal of winning the lottery he is probably under the illusion that if he had enough money all his problems could be solved. Examining this belief has interesting results for most people. Many discover that happiness is not created by wealth or destroyed by poverty.

In a Life Coaching Relationship 'I want to win the lottery' would not be accepted as a realistic goal because it is an outcome over which the client has little control. It is a goal that many people can relate to and few will have examined in any depth. It is a positive goal that carries with it the anticipation of a positive outcome which can be realised but it is not realistic. An achievable goal is something you get through your own efforts and you must control the outcome.

I need hardly tell you that millions of people want to win the lottery. The outcome depends on chance. The only aspect the client can control is that he can buy a ticket each week. As the advertisements say if he is not in he can't win. 'What would you have to do in order to win?' or 'How would you go about winning the lotto?' are questions that encourage the client to be realistic. 'What else?' might encourage him to look at other options like being part of a syndicate.

My purpose in continuing with the example of pursuing the concept of winning the lottery is that it is an excellent illustration for helping readers understand the benefits of coaching. I have already explained that this is an exercise that I would not do with a client because winning the lottery is not a realistic goal even though it is achievable.

I will use this example of the coaching process to demonstrate the limitations of trying to be your own coach. In order to work towards a well-formed outcome clients need to be challenged to broaden their thinking. Your thinking makes perfect sense to you. So how could you be objective or challenge yourself?

Depending on how motivated you are to benefit from this book you may want do the practical exercises on your own and you will benefit from this way of working. You may want to work with someone who will read out the questions. If they have the listening skills to reflect back what you say that will be very useful.

The challenge of working with a Life Coach is that she will listen, reflect, ask questions, challenge poorly thought out answers and suggest ways to reframe outmoded thinking. The insights that a client comes to during this process empower him to make decisions which are holistic and take account of the whole person and the lifestyle that fits his personal beliefs and values.

All of this preliminary goal setting may seem unnecessary when you are simply reading about the theory. It will probably make more sense when you understand how it works out in practice.

These are the client's two goals:

1. I want to win the lottery.
2. I want to understand the impact that having millions will make on my life.

Coach: I want you to find your positive reasons for wanting this goal? For what purpose do you want this?

Client: • I want to be rich.
   • I won't have to worry about paying my bills.
   • I can buy anything I want for my family and friends.
   • I can have exotic holidays and travel the world.

Coach: Anything else?

Client: I will:
   • never again have to worry about money.
   • be able to afford to buy everything I want.
   • clear my loans and debts.
   • build the house of my dreams.
   • be without a mortgage.
   • buy a car.
   • get a designer wardrobe.
   • bring my family on exotic holidays.
   • eat in expensive restaurants.

Coach: Describe what you will see, hear, feel etc.. Make it real
          for yourself.

Client: • I will wear designer clothes.

          • I will live in a mansion.

          • I'll have surround sound in every room.

          • I'll have a heated swimming pool.

          • I will eat, drink and be merry.

Coach: What will you lose when you get this?

Client: I will lose;

          • Poverty.

          • anxiety over paying my bills.

          • economy holidays.

Doesn't all of this sound wonderful? There is no denying that
there are many benefits that go with the initial euphoria of being
rich. In order to discover if being a lottery winner will have
longer term benefits and will have a positive effect in the longer
term the coach will have to probe a little more. She will want to
explore more challenging questions like;

Coach: I noticed that your were on your own in that dream
          fantasy. Perhaps it would be good to look and see how
          balanced your life would be with that change in lifestyle

          When you lose poverty what will you gain?

Client: • I'll feel great.

          • Life will be wonderful when I am rich and lose
            poverty.

- I can do anything I ever wanted to do.

- I can buy anything I want without worrying about my overdraft.

- All my problems will disappear.

- I can treat my friends and bring them places they never dreamed of going.

- Paying bills will be easy.

- Anxiety about money will be non-existent.

- I will travel first class.

GET REAL

All the answers are positively oriented and many of them need to be challenged. Why? There is a downside to every successful outcome that must never be ignored. Having enormous amounts of money will change more than a bank balance. It will change one's lifestyle and the spin-off effect is that will change one's relationships. Almost every aspect of one's personal and professional life will be affected because change is never an isolated occurrence. Enormous change in the financial area will put other areas out of balance.

It is not widely recognised that there is a price to pay for every change we make in our lives. Change is not self-contained. A successful achievement in one area of your life will have an impact on more than your life. When you introduce change in one area that change will have a knock-on effect for better or worse on your own life and on the lives of people who are close to you.

In coaching the client learns that in order to have a well-formed outcome he must be aware that any gain is always balanced with loss. This may be difficult to accept. Every time you gain something, some aspect of your life has to change. You lose something. It may be something that you want to lose or it may be a loss that will have a ripple effect on not just yourself but on many other people as well.

It may seem strange to think that a lottery winner may suffer by having money but that is the reality. Initially clients find it easy to identify what they will gain when they get the outcome they want. Unless they also look at what they will lose and name the loss or losses they cannot be sure that what they want is worthwhile.

Finding the balance involves examining the whole picture. Potential benefits always involve self and others. A vitally important question to ask when you are clarifying your goals is how will your changed circumstances change you and impact on your family and other relationships?

DEVIL'S ADVOCATE

So let me demonstrate how a coach challenges the client and helps him to get an overview of both the short and longer-term consequences of the outcome he thinks he wants.

Coach: 'Have you considered that it is only the very exceptional person who does not radically alter his lifestyle when he gets rich. Most lottery winners alter their lifestyles. if you win how would you see your relationships and social life change? So use your imagination now and fantasise about what it would feel like?

Imagine you have won the lottery. Put whatever figure you like on it, five, ten, twenty million, whatever.

- Feel what it is like to be rich.
- Create the whole scene in your mind.

- Where are you living?

- How do you spend your day?

- What do you do from the time you get up in the morning?

- See yourself going through the whole day.

- What do you eat?

- Who makes your meals?

- How do you occupy your time?

- Who do you spend time with?

- Where you are living?

- Who are your friends?

EXPLORE THE CHANGES

You can afford entertainment for your more financially challenged friends that they could never afford. You can take them to expensive restaurants or clubs. This will be very satisfying and make you feel good but after a while do you think that will change? Do you think you might begin to resent it if your friends have expectations that you will always pick up the tab? Do you think that they might feel under a compliment to you if you bring them places they can't afford? As a rich man would you be happy to accept hospitality from a friend who is struggling financially?

It's important when you are setting any goal to work out how you imagine your circumstances will change and how you and others will respond to those changes. Say you are wealthy and won an enormous amount of money. Will they have expectations of how you share your winnings? Many lottery winners who have been interviewed in the media say that their families change.

Do you think that the relationships you enjoy with your family and friends will stay the same? Check it out in your fantasy. Does money make a difference?

As a coach I would say to a client that it may not be his intention to allow his money to alter any relationship. 'You will still be the same person in your own eyes but others will relate to you in a new way. Your life situation will change radically. Family and friends will have expectations about what you should and should not do with your winnings. You will have become a 'Have' while they remain 'Have nots.' Even in the best of families envy and jealousy rear their ugly heads. Think about how you would cope in that situation. Would money compensate for the changes?'

At the end of the exercise it doesn't really matter what the client decides. The sole purpose of the exercise is for him to look at the whole picture and to make a decision that is right for him. The benefits of having a coach or friend ask curious questions is that the client is encouraged to focus and think and re-think the same issues.

WILL I PAY THE PRICE?

It is worth the client's time to check out how he thinks reaching the goal will make his life happier. As a coach I would invite him to be specific. 'You will want to weigh up all the pros and cons in order to clarify whether this altered lifestyle and changed relationships is really what you want.'

So continuing with the example of coming into big money let's demonstrate how the coach would explore the price to be paid.

'Your personal values and beliefs about money will play a major role in any decision you make. You can learn from every stage of this process. You may discover that your relationships with your family and friends are more important than you previously believed. Or you may find that you would be happy to leave your past behind and start afresh in a new environment and make a new life for yourself.'

The deeper insights that come from working with a Life Coach who understands you and holds you to account for answers that seem incongruent have to be experienced to be appreciated. Let's say a client decides to make a new life for himself. He claims that this is a positive goal with positive outcomes and worth wanting. His coach agrees with him and also recognises that there are other issues from which he is running away.

A competent coach will be fine tuned to pick up on unrealistic thinking, self-deception and issues that the client may not want to face. A person who wants to start a completely new life will have reasons that make sense to him. The techniques she would use to get a lottery winner to decide on a well-formed outcome will be equally useful in exploring any outcome a client wants.

MAKING A NEW LIFE

The coach will never appear to be judgemental. She understands that the client always has a positive reason for his actions that makes sense to him. By incisive questioning and challenging she will often help the client think things out again. Every client has resources that he doesn't use. In order to make the changes he wants he needs to become aware of how he stops himself from achieving his goals.

For some clients this is easy. They learn quickly. Once they reframe and think in a positive way they find they are energised and motivated. For others change is more difficult. They may have endured perceived failure and they find it difficult to develop new skills or training. Understanding how to achieve your desired outcome will only create change for those who believe that they can make changes.

Whatever you believe becomes true for you. Whether you are an optimist or a pessimist there is one important question every client needs to ask. What could go wrong? Working on your own this is not an easy question to answer. We have already seen that your attitude has a huge impact on the results you achieve. You want to have a positive belief about every decision you make. The coach will encourage you to look at everything that could help or hinder. By answering 'What could go wrong?' the client is challenged again. 'What if' questions are a most useful tool in getting the client to think about making contingency plans.

Imagine you read the words 'A cardboard box on a table.' As you read those words you mind is creating an image of a box on a table. The image may be in black and white or in colour. It may be life-size or bigger or smaller than life-size. It will have a location in a space. You will have thoughts about the box and may wonder why I want you to create the picture of a cardboard box, rather than a tin or wooden one.

As you think about the box what if you made it bigger? What is the response in you? If it is black and white what if you made it coloured? What is the response in you? If it is coloured what if you made it black and white? What is the response in you? What if you made it smaller? What is the response in you?

Do you get the idea? Every time you think of making a change you become aware of something different, don't you? You probably also become aware of thoughts or associations that the box evoked in you. In some cases the association will be connected or linked to a memory. In others the thought that comes into your mind defies logic and makes no sense to you.

It's really worth putting time aside to examine and work in depth with every outcome you desire. When you do so you may be astonished at the result. You are likely to discover that one part of you wants something and another part of you sabotages you and stops you from getting what you think you want. Or you may be surprised to discover that when you explore the consequences of getting the outcome you think you want you find the price is too high.

You can find out if you are ready to deal with the life-changing consequences of any decision by asking the following questions.

EXERCISE: CHECKING THE CONSEQUENCES

Write out your positive goal.

_____

_____

What will this outcome do for me?

_____

_____

_____

_____

_____

_____

Picture yourself with this outcome. I will see...

_____

_____

_____

_____

_____

_____

Picture yourself with this outcome. I will hear…

_____

_____

_____

_____

_____

Picture yourself with this outcome. I will feel…

_____

_____

_____

_____

_____

_____

What will feeling like this do for me?

_____

_____

_____

_____

_____

_____

How will that impact on work and career?

_____

_____

_____

_____

_____

_____

How will that impact on family?

_____

_____

_____

_____

_____

How will that impact on social life?

_____

_____

_____

_____

_____

_____

How will that impact on money?

_____

_____

_____

_____

_____

_____

How will that impact on fun and recreation?

_____

_____

_____

_____

_____

_____

How will that impact on self-care?

_____

_____

_____

_____

_____

How will that impact on health?

_____

_____

_____

_____

_____

_____

How will that impact on spirituality?

_____

_____

_____

_____

_____

What will I gain when I achieve this goal?

_____

_____

_____

_____

_____

_____

What will I lose when I achieve this goal?

_____

_____

_____

_____

_____

_____

What could go wrong?

_____

_____

_____

_____

_____

_____

Weary traveller complaining about planners: 'Why in the name of heaven did they decide to build the railway station three miles away from the town?'

Helpful porter: 'They must have thought that it would be a good idea to have it near the trains.'

SUMMARY

- Do you control your own goals?

- Questions that challenge you to rethink.

- Gain is always balanced with loss.

- Use your imagination and senses.

- See the whole picture before you make a decision.

'The way to use life is to do nothing through acting. The way to use life is to do everything through being'.

LAO TZU

CHAPTER 6

NEURO LINGUISTIC PROGRAMMING (NLP)

IN THIS CHAPTER:

- **Understand how you think.**
- **Use language to reach your goals.**
- **How to change your thinking and transform your life.**
- **Thoughts have a structure.**

'As long as a man stands in his own way, everything seems to be in his way.'
Ralph Waldo Emerson (1803 – 1882)

Two women friends met after many years, 'Tell me what happened to your son?' said one. 'My son, the poor unfortunate lad,' sighed the other. 'What an unfortunate marriage he has made – to a hussy who won't do a bit of work in the house. She won't cook. She won't work. She won't wash or clean. All she does is sleep and take it easy and read in bed. My poor boy even has to bring her breakfast in bed. Would you believe it?'

'That's awful! And what happened to your daughter?'

'Well she's the lucky girl. She married a wonderful husband. He won't let her do a thing in the house. He has someone come in to do the cooking and washing and cleaning. She doesn't have to lift a finger.'

'And each morning he brings her breakfast in bed. Would you believe she is so well taken care of? All she does is relax and read in bed.'

> *Where there is true understanding there is no problem.*
>
> Anthony de Mello

WHAT IS NEURO LINGUISTIC PROGRAMMING (NLP)?

Neuro Linguistic Programming (NLP) is a brilliant and powerful model for communication, personal growth and achievement of our potential as human beings.

NLP has found its way into sales training, business, therapy, sports, teaching, coaching and almost every area of personal excellence you wish to mention.

Founded on the modern sciences of biology and linguistics it explains how we create and maintain our inner thoughts and feelings. It offers simple techniques to create rapport with others and draw on mental resources. The 'Neuro' part refers to the nervous system. It explains the mental pathways of your five senses by which you see and hear and smell and taste and touch.

'Linguistic' refers to the ability to use Language. The linguistic part involves understanding how specific words and phrases mirror your mental world. You can learn to use language in very specific ways to help you reach your goals. Linguistic also refers to body language – postures, gestures and habits that communicate your styles of thinking and more.

The 'Programming' part is borrowed from computer science. Your thoughts, feelings and actions run like habitual programs in your brain. Just like you can upgrade and change computer programs you can change your mental programs. You already know how to do this. You change your mind. You learn to think in a different way.

Understanding a little about the background of NLP will help you achieve your personal goals. The principles and techniques are not difficult to understand or practice. This is why it is so widely used in Life Coaching. The emphasis is on doing and experiencing rather than on learning theory.

When you understand what is not working and why, you can change your actions or behaviour. Like the man at a bar who turned to the stranger sitting next to him and said, 'I just don't understand it. All it takes is one little drink, just one little drink to make me drunk.' 'Really?' asked the stranger, 'Just one?' 'Yes,' he replied, 'And it is generally the eighth one.'

The name NLP comes from the three areas it brings together; Neurology, Linguistics and Programming. It's based on principles that are very different from traditional psychology. Clinical psychology is primarily concerned with what, how and why things go wrong with people. Trainer Charles Faulkner says 'If we could summarise all the NLP pre-suppositions in one phrase it would be: People work perfectly.'

The founders of NLP were interested in discovering how our thoughts, actions and feelings produce our experiences. They discovered new ways of understanding how the human brain works and created new possibilities for achieving human excellence.

Once we understand how we think and why we respond as we do to our own thinking we are empowered to make choices. Our thoughts have a structure. When we change the structure we change many other aspects of what we think and do as well. NLP offers you a new way of looking at life. It gives you the tools that lead to change.

Some clients are so motivated to succeed that they are willing to move out of their comfort zones and deal with the discomfort of change. I can offer you the tools to change how you think. I can invite you to model a successful person that you admire or whose skills you value. I can't do it for you. You have to be willing to do the work yourself.

Many clients who work with a Life Coach have issues around success that appear to be illogical until they learn from NLP how they represent and interpret events. Or they are highly sceptical of the claims that they will be helped to understand how to create rapport and find workable solutions with difficult colleagues by simply changing how they communicate.

Some people are put off by jargon. They are born sceptics who want every 'i' dotted and every 't' crossed. They want a definition of NLP and when I admit that I'm not willing to try and define it in one specific way they become even more cynical.

Some of the many definitions I like that describe NLP are;

- 'The art and science of personal excellence.'
- 'The study of human excellence.'
- 'The study of subjective experience' and
- 'A simple skilful method to explore what goes on inside a person.'

All of these definitions are true and worthy of expansion. As you read on you will understand why they are all useful aids to understanding NLP and why it is impossible to pin it down to a single definition.

HISTORY OF NLP

In the 1970's anthropologist Gregory Bateson had a big influence on John Grinder and Richard Bandler who were both incredibly clever people. John Grinder was teaching linguistics at the University of California at Santa Cruz. Richard Bandler was a student of mathematics and information technology, with a special interest in psychology.

Bandler edited Gestalt therapy scripts to earn some money. He was excited by the structure of what the therapist was doing to create successful change in clients. Grinder also had an interest in psychology and personal change. Discovering their similar interests they decided to combine their respective talents. They set about uncovering 'The hidden grammar of thinking and acting' that is fundamental to the goal of linguistics.

They studied Dr Fritz Perls the German psychiatrist and Bandler went as far as imitating everything he saw Perls do. In the beginning he led a Gestalt Group each Tuesday for students and local people. He modelled himself on Dr Fritz Perls by doing exactly what he saw him do. He grew a beard, chain smoked and spoke English with a German accent. A few days later on Thursdays, Grinder would lead another group using the same verbal and non-verbal patterns of Dr Perls that Bandler used.

They systematically set out to find what made Dr Perls different from other less effective therapists. First they copied everything he did. Then they started to omit what they thought didn't work like the accent and the smoking until they found the essence of his techniques. This is how the discipline of Modelling Human Excellence began.

They also studied Virginia Satir one of the great founders of Family Therapy and Dr. Milton Erickson, M.D., the founder of the American Society of Clinical Hypnosis. They found that when they modelled what these great therapists did they could get similar results. When they 'Stepped into someone else's shoes' and mimicked what they did, they got similar results. They discovered that if one person can do something anyone can learn to do it.

Encouraged by their success they became a team and went on to do further research. Their college classes and evening groups attracted larger and larger attendances. Students eager to learn this new technology of change flocked to their lectures. The rest is history.

SPEED UP LEARNING

By observing excellence in other people and adopting their successful strategies and skills it was possible to speed up the process of learning. There are many sceptics who challenge the concept of modelling success. They believe that some people are born with God-given talents and natural abilities. These are the high achievers. They excel because of their superior abilities.

Now I would not for a moment deny that some people appear to have to work less hard to achieve excellence. However I do challenge the out-dated thinking about so-called 'Superior abilities.' Until the 1950's it was widely believed that only people with a natural talent could be elegant skiers.

Skiers strapped on a pair of skis and tried to follow more experienced skiers down the slopes. Their main instruction was to keep their skis from crossing over each other. Then some black and white 16mm films of skilled skiers in the Alps were studied frame by frame. The researchers watched every tiny movement elegant skiers made. They identified and divided the smooth motions of the skiing into what they called 'Isolates.'

They discovered that although elegant skiers had different styles they all used the smooth motions they called 'Isolates.' When beginners and average skiers were shown how to do these 'Isolates' they immediately improved. When they imitated the techniques that good skiers did naturally, the improvements were quick and dramatic.

In skiing the key to change for those who were not recognised as having natural talent began when they were taught to use the right muscles in the right way. In NLP the potential for change is extended to every part of a person's experience, physical, mental, emotional, and spiritual. You can observe excellence, adopt the successful strategies and skills used and you will speed up your own process of learning.

Generally speaking it takes about two generations for something new to become widely accepted. Today the applications of NLP turn up everywhere. The revolutionary approach to personal development and human communication has changed thinking. The astonishing discovery that by changing how you think you can transform what you think offers life-changing possibilities.

It has been proven time and time again that change that is induced as a result of willpower rarely lasts. If I lie in bed unable to sleep willpower will do nothing for my insomnia. If I use my mind to imagine a scene where I am in pleasant surroundings, feeling relaxed my body will respond to that imagery. My muscles will relax. I may not fall asleep but I will be more rested as a result of that experience.

Your mind is powerful. When you change your thinking you change your feelings. It's not the situation but how you make meaning of the situation that makes it pleasant or unpleasant for you. What is considered overcrowding in a train is seen as atmosphere in a nightclub. Isn't it amazing to think that your brain responds to what you believe is true? You think too many people in a train make for an uncomfortable environment and you're right. You think that lots of people crowded together in a nightclub make for a great atmosphere and your brain produces the feelings that reflect that belief.

When you use the brain the way it's designed to be used it is a powerful tool for change. You get new perspectives when you change your internal images. You have different physical and emotional responses.

Think of a lemon using all your sensory acuity. Imagine seeing that lovely round yellow object. In your mind feel the texture of the skin. Smell the skin of the fruit. Be aware of your bodily responses. Cut it in half. Think about tasting the lemon and your mouth will water. If you don't like bitter fruit you will probably grimace.

Things are as big or as small as your mind chooses to make them. A diamond is a stone until endowed with value by the human mind. The power of this change in perception is one of the most exciting things about using NLP. When you work on a one-to-one basis with a coach there are endless possibilities for opening your mind to new experiences. You will learn strategies for motivation, confidence, self-esteem, creativity and more.

SUMMARY

- **Tools to change how you think.**
- **Modelling success.**
- **Get a new perspective – change your internal images.**

'Watch your thoughts; they become words. Watch your words; they become actions. Watch your actions; they become habits. Watch your habits; they become character. Watch your character; it becomes your destiny.' –

FRANK OUTLAW

CHAPTER 7

VALUES

IN THIS CHAPTER:

- **Your values and beliefs guide the changes you make.**
- **Identify your values.**
- **Double standards.**
- **Why do you act as you do?**
- **Recognise outdated thinking.**

The Chief Executive Officer of a large company was greatly admired for his energy and drive. But he suffered from one most embarrassing weakness; each time he entered the Chairman's office to make his weekly report he would loudly pass wind that made a terrible smell.

The kind-hearted Chairman suggested that he see a consultant about his problem. When he came to report to the Chairman the following week he still farted. 'Didn't you see the specialist?' asked the Chairman.

'No, he was out. I saw a psychologist instead. I'm cured. I no longer feel embarrassed.'

YOUR BELIEFS CREATE SUCCESS OR FAILURE.

Your unconscious mind plays a part in everything you do. Your values and beliefs have a powerful impact on what you accomplish. They can generate a spiral of success or failure because what you believe is likely to become true for you.

Your values are the internal rules you have about how you and others should behave. You have beliefs about appropriate standards and you may not even be aware you have them. You have strong feelings about how things should be done and who should do them. You can also call these beliefs about standards and behaviours your values. Beliefs and values are the internal rules by which you live.

Your values suggest to your unconscious mind what you want to do. Your beliefs guide the choices you make. If you say 'I'm good at organising' you have a belief that empowers you to recognise and use a skill. If you say the opposite it is incredibly damaging. 'I'm no good at organising' damages self-esteem, knocks confidence and is probably untrue.

From NLP you know that there is no mystery about why you do not achieve what you are capable of achieving. People have mental filters that play an important role in how they interpret and make meaning of life events. These filters are formed by their memories, perceptions of past events, beliefs about what happened and why, and their values.

You are probably aware that you have a unique and subjective way of perceiving the world around you. Your experience in any situation is based on what you see, hear and feel. Another person in a similar situation will have a different response. What she sees and hears may be identical to what you see and hear but you will each have different feelings and emotional responses. Why? It's because you have different ways of filtering information. You literally make meaning in a way that is unique to you because your interpretation of events happens in the context of your life experiences.

IDENTIFYING YOUR VALUES

Your beliefs and values are important because they have an influence on what you think and what you do or don't do. I want to help you to identify your values in order to understand how they affect your goals and outcomes. In the process you will have insights about what motivates your actions.

Any decision you make that goes against your personal value system will create internal conflict. Your values are the rules you live by and if you are like many of us you may find that what you consider your values are not yours. They are inherited. In a moment I will ask you to take the time to identify your values. It's so easy that young children find it an easy task. It's also an enjoyable exercise because you will find interesting insights that will explain why you respond and react as you do.

I have worked with ten and eleven years old children who amazed me with their ability to discuss their values and beliefs. I was facilitating relationship education. I had the children form groups of four to six and elect a scribe for the group. Their task was to make a list of all the qualities they believed were important in friendship. When they were finished the elected scribe read out the list and I wrote it on the board.

If a quality was repeated I put an asterisk beside the word. That way we also identified the qualities that were generally more valued. If I had gone into the classroom and said I was doing a Values Clarification Exercise the children would not have understood what I was talking about. When I used words that they understood they were brilliant.

I have facilitated workshops with adults and invited them to do a similar exercise and have never had such a comprehensive list. When I told the children that I was writing for adults and asked permission to use their list as an example of what children can do they were thrilled.

VALUES AND BELIEFS

Trust

Love

Care

Kindness

Respect

Have things in Common

Communicate

Willing to share

Able to talk

Do things with others

Socialise

Co-operate

Be fair

Loyalty

Honesty

Humour

Generosity

No secrets

Helpful

Cheerful

Agree

Protect them

Understanding

Be friendly

Laughter and fun

Give presents

Faith

Surprises

Conversations

Feel comfortable

Memories

Advice

No arguments

Don't fight

Have a good time

Be nice to others

Honour

Remember birthdays

Have chats

Send postcards/text/ e-mails

Personality

Joy

Courage

Play

Don't rob

Keep promises

Think before you act

Stick together

Sincerity

Thank others

Mannerly

Don't bully

Play with younger people

Play with others who have

different views

Warm-blooded

I'm inviting you to go on a personal adventure in order to discover the beliefs that guide the choices you make. You will find out so much about where the important influences in your life originated. It is fascinating to look at different areas of your life and tune in to what you believe is important and why. In the process it is very likely that you will find that your behaviour is limited by inherited values that are not yours. You may wonder where some beliefs come from and discover that they belong to parents or teachers. It's likely that you will find that you are affected by values that are not even yours – for good or ill.

You may also make some discoveries about double standards. I suspect that you will find that you have an acceptance of spin. Many of us accept the manipulation of facts in the wheeling and dealing of business. Lies that would be deplored in a personal relationship are accepted in another context. They are excused because this is business. For example you may believe that honesty is important. Then you find you value it in personal relationships but in a business context your standards of integrity change.

You create your values and beliefs over a lifetime. I'm using 'Beliefs and values' interchangeably here. They affect all the outcomes you set for yourself and every decision you make. I want you to do an exercise that will bring up very important insights. You are likely to make discoveries and gain insights that will help you understand yourself and why you act as you do. Insights about internal conflicts that you felt but never understood can bring clarity to situations that have been a thorn in your side for years.

EXERCISE: WHAT IS IMPORTANT TO ME?

This is an exercise that you will need to have tenacity and determination to complete. I invite you to pick a time to write when you will not be interrupted. Give yourself as much time as you need. It may be wise to do one part of the exercise and have a break before going on to another part.

For this exercise you will need loose pages and coloured markers. Please write your answers for each heading on a separate page.

What is important to me about;

1. My work and career?

2. My family?

3. My social life?

4. Money?

5. Fun and recreation?

6. Self-care?

7. Health?

8. Spirituality?

Get out your coloured markers. Go back over what you have written and find your values and beliefs. Your answers will probably include values like; 'Love,' 'Making a contribution,' 'Respect,' 'Satisfaction,' 'Having fun,' 'Making money' and so on. Circle them with a coloured marker. Some values will recur in every area of your life. It's useful to put a second circle around them with a different coloured marker.

Make a list of the values you have circled. For each value ask the question, 'Why do I believe that this is important for me?'

VALUES   WHY IS THIS IMPORTANT TO ME?

_____   _____

_____   _____

_____   _____

_____   _____

_____   _____

_____   _____

_____   _____

_____   _____

_____   _____

_____

Try to use single words or very short phrases. Your answers will reflect the values you hold in each of those areas. Keep your answers short. Be self-aware as you do this. Your first response is usually a spontaneous and honest answer. If you find yourself stuck for an answer or you can't find the appropriate word it may mean that you have to reconsider the value.

Now go back to the Wheel of Life Exercise and re-read what you wrote. Find the values and beliefs that motivated you to enjoy the different parts of your life. You will find that those answers will confirm the values you have listed and may bring up other values you hadn't thought about. Don't be surprised to find that many of the same values keep cropping up again and again. Take a break when this task is finished. You now have clarity about your values.

BENEFITS OF THE EXERCISE

The benefit of an exercise like this is that it will challenge you to discover any contradictions between what you believe you value and what your behaviour shows you actually value. You will find that some values are important to you in one context and not so important in others.

The benefit of working with a coach is that she will pick up on any contradiction between your stated goals and values. She may challenge you to identify values you had not thought about.

She will want you to explain what you mean when you say that you value 'Security' or 'Respect.' In the process of explaining what any value means to you and why it is important you will find that you are challenged to think about the contexts in which you want 'Love' or you want to 'Make a contribution.'

The discipline of answering slightly different questions about the same topics will help you to be very specific. It's exciting to become aware of what you believe in today and why you need to let go of old outdated thinking that holds you back.

MIND READING

Any time you believe that you can tell what someone else is thinking you are acting on an assumption that is not valid. Mind reading is a belief that you can know what another person is thinking or feeling or be tuned in to what motivates the other without asking or consulting him. You can't know what someone else is thinking but you can make an educated guess.

I'm reminded of the two travelling salesmen who met on the platform of a railway station.
'Hello'

'Hello'

Silence.

'Where are you off to?'

'Galway'

Silence.

'Listen! When you say you're going to Galway you know that I'll think you're actually going to Donegal. But I happen to know that you are going to Galway. So why don't you tell the truth?'

Mind reading is the cause of much conflict and miscommunication. It can prevent a person from reaching his goals. It's almost impossible to challenge your own mind reading. For example a man may think 'Bobbie doesn't like me.' Without checking if this is true he withdraws. Bobbie is a shy woman. The man responds to the belief he has about her. He makes an assumption and acts as if it is a fact.

Our beliefs are very powerful. A coach will encourage the client to clarify what he is thinking and check for distorted or mistaken thinking. You have an emotional response to what you tell yourself, not to reality. In the coaching relationship the client is empowered to achieve new insights by thinking the unfamiliar.

The coach will help the client to find a different perspective by asking questions that challenge him to see things in a different way. For example, if a coach were working with the man who believed that Bobbie didn't like him, she would ask him 'How specifically do you know that?' She will help him to become aware of any mind reading or guesswork.

In this process the client will learn that his response is to his own beliefs. He creates a story to explain the assumptions he made about Bobbie. He believes and responds to his own mental construction of the situation, not to reality.

It is vitally important for you to understand that your feelings are your own emotional response to how and what you think. Despite all the modern advances in science we cannot really know how anyone else thinks and we certainly cannot know what another person feels.

INHERITED VALUES.

In a one-to-one coaching relationship clients frequently discover that they are powerfully influenced by a value system that they have inherited from their parents. When you read your list of values you may find that you have outgrown some and that it would be wise to reconsider others. You will gain useful insights into your value system by going back to the source. 'Where did that come from?' will illustrate the random origins of beliefs that inhibit you from setting or achieving your goals.

Your values present you with negotiable choices. In every situation your internal response is influenced by how you choose to think about the event. Beliefs that you have accumulated historically may have served you well in the past. By identifying and reappraising your present-day beliefs you create choices based on your present desires, goals and values.

We can and do change our values and beliefs over time. Usually we have strong reasons for holding onto old beliefs, even when they do not serve us well. A strong value will suggest to your unconscious mind what you want. So when you do any work on setting your goals you want to become aware of how the values and beliefs you hold affect what you want and how you plan to achieve the outcomes you desire.

Questions that someone who wants to change career might ask would include, 'What's important about my career?'

'I'd like to work in a bank or be a teacher or writer, whatever.'

'What's important about working in a bank or being a teacher, secretary, writer, whatever?'

Answers would include, 'Getting paid,' 'Respect for my professionalism,' 'Job satisfaction,' 'Meeting clients' and so on. The answers you give reflect your values. You may even find it helpful to ask seemingly obvious questions like 'Why is this important? Some of the replies may seem obvious. 'It's important to be paid so I have money to live.' 'Why is this important?'

It's like peeling an onion. You get one answer and you repeat the question and go beneath that and you find another insight. Your answers will uncover layers of understanding that will deepen your awareness of what you believe and really value.

Reflect on what you learn.

SUMMARY

- **Mind reading causes conflicts.**
- **Let go of outdated beliefs.**
- **List of values from 10 to 12 year-olds.**
- **Finding your own values.**

'To attain Knowledge,
add things every day.
To attain Wisdom,
remove things every day.'

Lao Tzu.

CHAPTER 8

SUCCESS HAS A PRICE

IN THIS CHAPTER:

- **Do you feel fulfilled?**
- **Learn to think in a new way.**
- **Opportunity is now.**
- **Believe in yourself.**
- **Bring balance to your life.**

*'To all seeking success – whether
their beliefs were political,
economic or religious it
mattered not – the Spiritual Master
had one message.*

*'What you need is not security
but the daring of the gambler,
not solid ground to stand on
but the dexterity of the swimmer.'*

Anthony de Mello S.J.

MOVING TOWARDS FULFILMENT AND BALANCE

Some people who have achieved excellence in some areas of their lives are not doing what they really want to do. They are fulfilling someone else's dreams for what they should be doing. Their parents or teachers decided that they should go for a certain career because they appeared to have an obvious aptitude. They become aware years later that they have achieved professional success at a job they don't enjoy and for which they have no passion.

Many clients who come for coaching are very successful in their professional lives. Yet they feel that there is something missing. They complain about an emptiness; a lack of satisfaction. It's not uncommon for a client who is very successful in his career to feel unfulfilled after the initial euphoria wears off. He seeks help because he can't figure out what is the problem. At one level he seems to have it all. He is earning good money, enjoys the perks and status that go with the job and despite this he is not happy.

His coach can quickly help him discover why. So often when a professionally successful client is missing a sense of personal fulfilment his life is out of balance. He is concentrating on some aspects and ignoring others and he is paying a price for that neglect.

Once a capable and resourceful client discovers why he feels like he does he has choices. He may decide on a change of career or he may choose to change his attitude. Either way he gets results. Each client is his own most important resource. Everywhere he goes he brings himself with him. These insights encourage the client to think in a new way. The result may be that he will do something that he may never have done before or he will continue to do what he has been doing with a new attitude. Whatever choice he makes his feelings will have changed and that is the difference that makes the difference.

In the coaching process the client is challenged to be honest with his feelings. Being emotionally honest is not easy. Most people take emotional dishonesty for granted. They lie to themselves without being aware of the internal tensions they are creating. A

coach can observe patterns in how a client thinks and behaves.
She can encourage him to become aware of unhelpful patterns of
behaviour and once he understands what he is doing to himself he
can move towards change and transformation.

When a client recognises old patterns of behaviour that no longer
serve him well he will be invited to explore more helpful ways of
dealing with situations and people. Coaching involves learning to
think in a new way. Some clients regret that they never had the
opportunity to do something or go someplace. They talk about
seizing opportunities when they arrive.

The opportunity to correct patterns of behaviour and generate
new ways of dealing with situations never arrives. It is already
here. You make the opportunity. You get an insight that helps
you understand something. You have new information that you
can plan to use starting NOW. The coach expresses confidence
that the client has all the answers. She knows that some clients
need support in making choices.

When you believe in yourself you will trust your own experience.
For some insecure clients self-trust is difficult. They need to
check things out before they are willing to act on a fresh insight.
The coach will be there to encourage such clients to take
responsibility for their own actions. Her belief is a powerful
catalyst for the client to find a workable solution. Phrases like
'Starting immediately what could you do?' show that the coach
has confidence in the client's ability to act now.

In Life Coaching the agenda in each coaching session is focused
on the client. The coach's role is to do whatever is necessary to
move the process ahead. She will get the client to have an
overview and to think about the whole picture. In order to work
towards his desired outcome the client needs to recognise how
important it is to have balance in his life.

Coaching is not counselling or therapy although it borrows from both. The coach is committed to the ultimate goals of the client. She will do whatever is necessary to help him. In the process she will use a variety of skills to keep her client on track. If she has to she will challenge, cajole, incite, motivate, encourage, push and make the client accountable for every success or failure in meeting targets.

I CAN'T DO THIS ON MY OWN

Many who say they want a significant life change feel they can't achieve it on their own. Coaching is one solution but it is not cheap. For some people the financial stakes are very high. They are investing in a future outcome based on a relationship where they do all the work and accept the total responsibility for success.

Coaching is a professional relationship that makes the client responsible for creating the outcome he desires. It is so successful because the experience of working with a mentor who is totally committed to the client and his agenda is most empowering and motivating.

Many very caring parents have the best of motives when they do what they believe is best for a child. In recent years we have the benefit of psychological insights that help us understand the damage that power struggles in families cause. It is not uncommon for a client to present with the goal of changing his career. He believes he had no choice about his career.

He did what was expected and followed in the footsteps of his father and maybe his grandfather too. So he went into the army or became a doctor or whatever happened to be the 'family' profession. With the help of intuitive questioning by his coach he may discover that his problem is not with the career but with his perception that it was decided on for him.

A lovely metaphor for situations like this is the story of the man who gave large doses of cod-liver oil to his pet dog. He read that the stuff was good for dogs and despite the unpleasant smell he persisted in feeding it to his pet. Each day he would hold the head of the protesting dog between his knees, force its jaws open and pour the medicine down its throat.

One day his pet broke loose and spilled the cod-liver oil on the floor. Then to the man's great surprise the dog licked it off the floor and returned to lick the spoon. That is when he found out that what the dog had been fighting was not the medicine but his method of administering it.

INTAKE SESSION

When you read about the intake session in coaching it may sound rather ordinary and not very impressive. Yet those who have had the experience say it is amazing to sit with a person who is totally focused on listening to everything you say as if it is the most important revelation in the world. An empathetic listener creates an atmosphere of acceptance and respectful exchange. That experience of being fully accepted for who you are allows an honest appraisal of where you are at, what are your qualifications, talents and personal resources and what you really feel you want from your life and relationships.

Unless you have had personal experience of being with someone who shows a genuine interest in everything you say you can have no concept of what the intake session in coaching is like. An experienced coach with NLP training develops rapport almost immediately. She listens to what is said and is tuned in to what is not said.

Many clients are amazed when a coach demonstrates such an understanding of his personality that she names some of the obstacles he sees in his way. This is not because the coach has mind-reading skills. As the client explains about his goals and dreams he will unconsciously give clues about what stops him achieving. A skilled coach is clued in to pick up the throw away remarks and focus in on the little asides that tell another part of his story. She picks up and comments on these.

A good communicator listens more than she speaks. She is tuned in to her client's body language. Her trained eye will pick up changes in breathing, hand gestures and eye movements that indicate emotional changes as the client talks.

My clients are often amazed that I seem to have such a deep understanding of what they are thinking and feeling. I don't deny that I have good intuition. I do deny that I am psychic. The explanation is quite ordinary. I am a skilled communicator trained in NLP.

Words are only a very small part of communication. A person's facial expression, tone of voice and body language communicates more than any words the client says.

TUNE INTO YOUR FEELINGS

When you are not at ease, when you are under pressure or you feel even a vague sense of dissatisfaction there is a genuine reason. You can be extremely successful in one area and still feel dissatisfied or even feel a total failure because something has not worked out the way you want. Dissatisfaction and success are not mutually exclusive.

When a person appears to be outwardly successful it is hard to admit that he feels dissatisfied. The tendency is to blame the self for feeling like this. A client will ask 'What is wrong with me? Why do I feel like this?' The blame frame is very familiar to us all. 'I should be happy with what I have achieved,' 'Why can't I just accept that this is good enough? I ought to be thrilled with what I have achieved.' Whatever the reason the client is dissatisfied and this dissatisfaction needs to be addressed.

Feelings are neither right nor wrong. When a person feels dissatisfied there is something that is disturbing him that needs attention. The wise man admits to himself that the outer trappings of success do not always make for a quality of life that fulfils and makes for happiness.

We all need to take time to explore what we think and feel about different aspects of our lives. When a client sees the whole picture he can look at where he is putting his energy in order to bring balance back into his life. Unless he takes that time to tune in to what he tells himself and how he responds to his own thinking he cannot have any insight into the root cause of why he feels unhappy or what is the reason for his dissatisfaction.

WE ARE ALL DIFFERENT

For one man the demands at work may contribute to feelings of loneliness and for another the identical demands may create feelings of achievement and satisfaction. The former has a desire to spend time with his family. The latter is glad of the excuse to spend time away from home. It's not the work situation but the man's reaction to it that makes it pleasant or unpleasant.

It's important to bear in mind that what satisfies a person at one time may not continue to do so. In the beginning a client enjoys the outer measures of a successful career. A great job, plenty of money, travel and expensive clothes creates a certain lifestyle that appears to be very exciting. It is at first and then the initial euphoria wears off. It is astonishing how quickly a person can get used to a particular lifestyle.

A few years later when the successful man has a family his priorities change. His wife enjoys their comfortable life-style but is unhappy that her husband is away from home so much. He misses his family and feels under pressure when his wife complains. Now that his circumstances have changed he finds that the perks of the job no longer satisfy or make up for the family times he misses when he is abroad.

To the father who values family life and wants to be at home to spend time with his children the external signs of professional success quickly lose their lustre. Over time as his family circumstance change his priorities change too. Commitments to keep his family in the style to which they have grown accustomed trap him in a job that once gave him everything he wanted and now no longer fulfils his needs. A growing unhappiness and dissatisfaction can affects many areas of life at work and at home.

Having a national profile or money in the bank or going on three foreign holidays a year are recognised signs of professional success but they do not necessarily make for happiness. Once the first flush of excitement is over and the client gets used to the higher standard of living he takes it for granted. It loses its attraction and is no longer very exciting. It's just what he has to do for a living.

The definition of job satisfaction is intensely personal. What is highly valued by one client may have little or no value for another. Clients have their own definitions of success that reflect their values and beliefs.

A fulfilled life involves work and family and leisure. There are many different parts in us and it is not uncommon for these parts to be in conflict. One part may delight in having a healthy bank balance while another part may feel guilty about having so much money.

A client may have attained a personal lifestyle of which his parents disapprove and that does not fit his family values. One part of him feels good and another part of him is angry that his achievement is devalued by his parents' disapproval. A client's personal values powerfully influence every decision that is made in a coaching relationship.

THE CLIENT IS ALWAYS RESPONSIBLE

A wrong understanding of coaching is that the coach is there to make things right for the client. She is not a problem solver. Her sole aim in the coaching relationship is to work with the agenda of the client. She will help him decide on realistic goals based on his strong motivation to succeed. She will encourage and support his plan to achieve his goals, get him to take responsibility for whatever action needs to be taken and agree on a time frame for completion of each step in the process.

This is what makes the coaching relationship such a powerful catalyst for change. The ongoing support of a mentor who respects that each decision the client makes has a purpose creates an understanding acceptance that is empowering. Few of us experience that level of total acceptance for what we think and do. When a client understands that his coach accepts that behind everything he says or does there is a positive intention that makes sense to him, he learns that he can be totally honest.

This support and encouragement is what makes the coaching relationship so worthwhile. You may be reading this book because you are contemplating a coaching relationship and you are not sure if it is a good investment. You will find a number of useful exercises in this book that I use with my clients. You will find many practical and useful suggestions that will help you work towards your desired goals.

Unfortunately no book, no matter how practical or well written it is can talk back to you. As an author of a book on coaching I am committed to helping you believe that you have all the resources you need to work towards and achieve your goals. I want you to feel challenged by the questions that I ask you to answer. Unfortunately I will not be around to give you the feedback that will encourage you to explore more deeply and find insights that will motivate you to move forward.

From past experience I know that many of my readers will simply read the exercises and not bother to write the answers as I suggest. There is nothing I can do about this other than to challenge the reader to consider the benefits of the insights he will miss out on by failing to do the suggested work.

Being encouraged to do the work in order to achieve realistic goals while being held accountable for each step in the process is one of the practical benefits of having a Life Coach. Many very gifted and talented people are not self-starters. They need to work with someone who will keep them on track and support them on the way to achieving a successful outcome.

I remember one client who had his heart set on working abroad for his company. He was prepared to do whatever it took to visit foreign countries. He found an opportunity when another colleague confided in him that he was scheduled to work abroad with an unpopular manager that had a reputation for being very narrow-minded. My client saw an opportunity and volunteered to go instead. His colleague was delighted and promptly accepted the offer.

'Was what you wanted worth having?' I asked. 'Yes and no,' he replied. 'I enjoyed the experience of working abroad but that guy's company spoiled the trip for me.' 'In what way?' I enquired. 'Travel should broaden the mind. He took every opportunity to broaden the area over which he spread his narrow-mindedness.'

SUMMARY

- **Perks and status are not always enough.**
- **Dissatisfaction and success are not mutually exclusive.**
- **The coach is not a problem-solver.**

'No problem ever comes to you for which the answer in not already within you'.

'You may depend on the inner mind absolutely. Everything you need to know will come to you when you need to know it'.

DR. EDWARD KRAMER.

CHAPTER 9

STRATEGIES FOR SUCCESS

IN THIS CHAPTER:

- **Understand your strategies.**
- **Change what's not working.**
- **Develop self-awareness.**
- **How am I?**

*A young author once told Mark Twain that he was losing
confidence in his ability to write.*
'Did you ever get that feeling yourself?' he asked.
*'Yes,' said Twain. 'Once, after I had been writing for nearly fifteen
years, it struck me that I did not possess the slightest talent for writing.'*
'What did you do then? Did you give up writing?'
'How could I? By then I was already famous.'

RECIPES FOR SUCCESS

Whether you achieve your goals or not depends solely on you and
the strategies you use. Make no mistake about this. You get
results because of what you do and how you do it. The recipe for
success works in a similar way to the recipe for making a cake.
Say you have a recipe for a wonderful chocolate cake. You collect
and weigh out the ingredients. You follow the recipe and mix the
ingredients together in the right order. You use the right size of
cake tin and bake the mixture at the correct temperature. You get
the same results each time you make the cake.

A strategy for success works in the same say. You start with the right ingredients. You use them in the right order. You get predictable results. Successful people have successful strategies. They think about the outcome they want. They imagine what they will have to do to achieve that outcome. Then they go ahead and do it. They become successful because they use the right strategies or recipes for success.

People who fail to do what they set out to do and who procrastinate have incompetent strategies. In NLP the term strategy usually means, 'a prepared mental programme leading to a specific outcome.' Your mental strategy is the key to whether you enjoy success or failure.

You have choices about any course of action you take. You probably begin with expectations that what you do will achieve a particular outcome. If you suffer with procrastination you may even consider whether or not you should bother to act. You may not even begin the process.

Procrastinators gain great benefit from the coaching relationship. In their past they said they wanted to act but didn't ever get around to beginning. Working with a Life Coach they choose to abandon old strategies that did not work. They do something different.

The coach will work with the client who used to be a procrastinator. She will be able to help him work with a strategy that will motivate him to get started. The well-deserved reputation that coaching has for getting quick results is due in part to clients wanting something different and being willing to discard old patterns of behaviour in favour of new strategies.

PROGRAMMING

If you're a self-starter you will need a strategy to motivate yourself and a follow up strategy to actually complete the task. The sequences of mental strategies you use has a powerful effect on whether you learn from your experiences or not.

You might like to think about the pair of hunters who chartered a plane to fly them into forest territory. Two weeks later the pilot came to take them back. He took a look at the animals they had shot and said, 'This plane won't take more than one wild buffalo. You'll have to leave the other one behind.'

'But last year the pilot let us take two in a plane this size,' the hunters protested. The pilot was doubtful, but finally he said 'Well, if you did it last year I guess we can do it again.'

The plane took off with the three men and two buffaloes. But it couldn't gain height and crashed into a neighbouring hill. The men climbed out and looked around. One hunter said to the other 'Where do you think we are?' The other inspected the surroundings and said 'I think we're about two miles to the left of where we crashed last year.'

Every mental programme you have has a huge impact on how you think and on the choices you make. Your programming creates a sequence of thinking and behaviours that you use like you would use a combination lock on a safe. When you use the same numbers in the same sequence you can predict the results.

I remember hearing about a drunk who was walking down the street with blisters on both of his ears. A friend asked him what had happened to cause the blisters. 'My wife left her hot iron on, so when the phone rang I picked up the iron by mistake.'
'Yes but what about the other ear?'
'The damned fool called back.'

When you consistently think how you always thought you will continue to do what you have always done. Guess what? You will consistently get the same results time after time after time. I hardly need to spell it out for you. When you always do what you have always done you always get what you have always got. If you are not happy with the results that you are getting you need to do something different.

The radio genius, Marconi, sat up all night with a friend in his laboratory discussing the intricate aspects of wireless communication. As they were leaving the laboratory Marconi suddenly said 'All my life I have been studying the matter but there is one thing I simply cannot understand about radio.' 'Something you do not understand about radio!' said the astonished friend. 'What is it?'
Said Marconi 'Why does it work?'

The good news is that once you understand why you think and behave as you do you have discovered the strategies you are using. As soon as you identify a problem you can begin to work towards the solution. Find the strategy that is not working for you. If you change one ingredient in how you approach a task it's like changing the recipe for a cake. You will get a different result.

This is simple to understand and harder to put into practice. It is easy to say that one strategy for problem solving is to change what is not working. It's not as easy as it sounds. I can suggest that you find the ingredients for change, use them in the right way and you will learn why the strategies you use work or don't work for you. It's useful to have the help of a coach for this process. A problem that is very obvious to a coach may stare a client in the face but he fails to see it because he is too close.

Even the simplest action involves complex strategies that consistently work toward success or failure. Understand what you do and how you do it so that you can keep the strategies that work well for you and change those that are not useful giving you the results you want. In order to change what is not working you need self-understanding and self-awareness. You need the spirituality of knowing who you are and how you are.

SELF-AWARENESS

You need self-understanding in order to become aware of the strategies you use in life. You need self-awareness in order to understand yourself and what you do and why you respond in your own unique way. How do you get self-understanding and self-awareness and how long will it take to get them?

If you are willing to discard old thinking that no longer serves you well you can start this minute. This sounds so simple that it almost seems too easy when you read the words. Are you willing to take a few minutes to sit with these questions and find the answers?

EXERCISE: HOW AM I?

Make sure you will not be interrupted when doing this exercise. Take the phone off the hook. Turn off your cellphone. Give yourself space and time.

Sit quietly in a comfortable chair for about 5 minutes first. See how you feel. Now gently bring your attention to your breath and stay with the awareness of breathing in and out. You'll be pleasantly surprised by how relaxing it is to just sit and become aware of your breathing. If you have attended a seminar on reducing stress you will be familiar with this kind of relaxation or meditation exercise. A small number of people find this kind of exercise unhelpful. When they slow down they can't handle the silence.

If you find it hard to stay with the awareness of your breath use another exercise. Get in contact with the physical sensations in your body instead. I suggest you bring your awareness to the top of your head and pay attention to any sensations you feel there. Then become aware of your face, neck and shoulders. Scan from the top of your head to the tip of your toes. This will slow you down. While you are concentrating on how you feel your thinking slows down. This quieter mind will help you relax.

After about 5 minutes when you feel relaxed and calm do the following exercise.

Please write two or three sentences about each heading.

How am I feeling physically?

_____

_____

_____

Are my thoughts and feelings connected?

_____

_____

_____

What will happen if I change my thinking?

_____

_____

_____

How will I feel if I change my thinking?

_____

_____

_____

Don't be at all surprised to discover that you need determination and strength of character to do this exercise. It is a form of meditation as well as a great relaxation exercise. If you are serious about being a successful person you will put time aside each day to develop your awareness. This is NOT, I repeat NOT, navel-gazing and it is not time wasting. It helps you to become aware of how you motivate yourself.

At the very least this exercise will help you relax. Just being willing to take time out to sit with yourself and to check out how you are will have a surprising level of stress reduction. I want you to experience the benefits of taking the time to become aware of your physical and emotional feelings. Your feelings are powerfully influenced by what you think. When you change what you think you change what you feel.

Some of my clients find this a difficult exercise. They are not used to being introspective. They come up with answers like:

Coach: How are you feeling physically?
Client: Physically I'm feeling fine.

Coach: What's your mood like?
Client: My mood is good.

Coach: What are you thinking?
Client: I'm not sure what I'm thinking?

Coach: There is often a connection between what you think to
         and how you feel?
Client: Is there a connection? I don't know!

In a face-to-face session the coach would help the client to tease out these questions. Finding the impact your thinking has on how you feel is the key to risk-taking and challenge. It opens up the client to new thinking and frequently the coach doesn't have to ask the final two questions. The client will already have discovered the answers. In a real-life coaching situation the benefits are immediate and obvious.

Let's say the client says he doesn't know what he is thinking. A coach might intervene in this way;

Coach: Just let yourself relax for a moment. Really pay attention to how you are feeling. Pay attention to whatever you are aware of this minute.

Client: Now that you ask me to do this I'm becoming aware of something. Physically I am feeling a little tired. I'm aware of tension in my shoulders. I've been sitting at the computer for too long without a break, probably.

Coach: You know how you feel physically. You have an explanation - so you can tell me why you think you feel that way. It is difficult at first to come up with the answer when I ask, 'What are you thinking?' Yet when you follow the process you get an answer.

You experienced tiredness and tension in your shoulders. You focused on the discomfort and found an explanation. Sounds like you were sitting at the computer for too long and this caused the tension in your shoulders. I'm curious about why you would do so?

Take time again to sit quietly and be aware of what happens in you.

Client: I'm not into this feeling stuff. I'm wondering if we are wasting time. I'm feeling impatient. I want to get on with it.

Coac: Seems like you identified lots of feelings there. You feel impatient at wasting time. Where did you learn how important it is to use time well?

Client: My father was a stickler for being on time and getting things done on time. He used to make us stick at tasks until we finished them, no matter how long it took us. We were never allowed to leave anything half-finished.

Coach: Is there any connection between believing you stick at a task until it is finished and the tension in your shoulders from sitting at the computer for too long.

Client: Probably. I never thought about it before but I probably should take regular breaks.

You can see how the client makes the connection and immediately thinks of a different strategy.

The coach will adapt the exercise when she is working face-to-face with a client. Once the client is aware of how he feels physically and emotionally he will come to a better understanding of what motivates him. The coach doesn't need to point out that the exercise was not a waste of time. The client experienced the benefit and arrived at the insight he needed to change and work more efficiently.

You probably never thought about the physical strategy you use to keep your body upright. You have a physical strategy to stand and other strategies to move your arms and legs. You know that it takes energy to keep your body upright. It takes physical power for you to stand and move the different parts of your body. You probably use these strategies and power all the time without thinking.

You also have emotional strategies. As you become more self-aware you will grow in understanding of how they impact on your behaviour and thinking. You will be surprised at the self-knowledge you gain and pleased as you get to know yourself better.

This is a brilliant exercise in self-awareness. Give it the time it deserves. You will find that it is a most effective way for you to understand the behaviours that lead you towards or away from the outcomes you desire. It takes time and a willingness to sit and become aware of what you feel. I cannot stress enough how worthwhile it is to do so.

SELF TALK

How you communicate with yourself and with family, friends and colleagues is the key to how you relate both to yourself and to others. It takes energy to communicate meaning. In this context a simple definition of communication is the giving and receiving of meaning. The meaning of communication is the response you get. If you are not getting the response you want your coach will help you to learn how to change your communication and to keep changing it until you get what you want.

Self-awareness involves learning to know yourself and to become aware of what you think and how you feel and even to have some sense of where those feelings originate. I'm serious about this. If you want balance in your life it is not enough to take the time to work with the goals you want to achieve. You also need to be aware of all the consequences that you can anticipate.

A client may tell me that there is tension in his body and he feels anxious thinking about what he has to do or what he has left undone. I cannot say whether this is a good or a bad thing for the client. Only he can say. A Sports Coach may want him to let go of the tension and relax. A Life Coach will work with the client where he is at. If anxiety will motivate him to move forward she will help him to use that anxiety in a positive way.

Another client may complain that he has no confidence in himself. Invited to say what he sees as his strengths he answers that he works hard. At the end of the session after doing the 'How am I?' his thinking has changed. His awareness of what he was doing to himself has altered and this change influences what he thinks and how he feels.

In the course of an hour he has gained new insights. He has gained fresh understanding that brings him to see what he does and why. He now has new choices and awareness of what he needs to do to feel secure, confident, capable, and comfortable with himself. He can take charge of his own life because he will no longer allow the voices of the past to control his actions.

Insights like this challenge and transform peoples' thinking. They learn how their own thinking limits their choices. Once they gain this insight they can take back their power. Life-changing insights happen in an instant. They literally bring about a new state of mind. For example a client who left school at fifteen with no formal qualification wants to work with children. He believes he has to go back to school and study for an art degree before he can do this.

His coach finds that he works as an artist. He has exhibited his work and sells many of his paintings She asks if there is any advantage in being self-taught. He gives her a list that include the originality of his work, self learning and the colourful results that came out of his experimentation with materials. Suddenly he has a change of mind about the lack of a degree. What he once believed was a disadvantage is now seen as an asset.

That insight changes everything for him. He now believes he will be okay. He recognises resources that can be marketed as his unique selling point. He can advertise with a healthy trust that people will respond to the creative posters he will use to demonstrate his artistic ability and talent.

A simple insight can make it acceptable for a client to recognise that he has courage, determination and the wisdom to talk himself out of playing old mind tapes that hold him back.

At one time people who talked to themselves were considered crazy. If your coach asks you to tell her 'What are you thinking right now?' you answer. If she then invites you to say how you are feeling, you would also give an answer. Now whether you are aware of it or not you talk to yourself in order to find those answers.

You have strategies for talking to and answering yourself that you use all the time. You're just not aware of how you use them. When you are learning to develop self-understanding and self-awareness your coach will invite you to take time out to slow down your thinking in order to become aware of the process or strategy you use.

Once you become aware of what you say to yourself it is only a small step to becoming aware of the feelings that show how you respond to thinking in the way you do. I need hardly tell you that if you don't like the feeling response you get you change what you are thinking until you are happy with the results. Doesn't this help explain how coaching works and why it has such quick results?

COMPETENCE

I'm not sure if you are aware that there are four stages you go through on the way to becoming competent working with a new strategy.

First you have unconscious incompetence. You haven't done the task before. You don't even know what if any parts of a task are important for you. You don't know that you don't know.

Second you have conscious incompetence. You know what you want to achieve but you don't yet have the skills to be good at achieving your outcome.

The third stage is conscious competence. You have now gained the skills you need but you still need to pay attention to how you use those skills.

The fourth and final stage is unconscious competence. You have now become so skilled that you can use the strategy automatically without having to think about how you do it.

For almost all of the things you do every day without thinking you have reached that level of unconscious competence. Mostly you work on automatic pilot and when your coach invites you to slow down and tell her how you do something you find it hard. Your unconscious competence is like a program in your brain that you rarely need to access.

The brain needs these programs in order for you to function. If you had to stop and think about the strategy you use to do everything you do in the morning from the time you wake up until the time you arrive at work you might be tempted to stay in bed. For the purpose of this exercise I am defining a strategy as 'A prepared mental program leading to a specific outcome.'

In the morning you have a prepared mental programme that works efficiently. You rarely give a thought to the strategies you use to; wake up, get out of bed, wash, get dressed, make breakfast, eat breakfast, put away the breakfast dishes, iron a shirt, leave the house and go to work.

You continue to produce the same results consistently day after day once your program conditions you to how the system works. You can evolve new strategies and get different results any time you want. It's your choice to decide what you want from every aspect of your life and to find a strategy to achieve those desires.

SUCCESS OR FAILURE

A Life Coach will work with her client to help him set goals. She will commit to support and encourage him to keep him on track. She will hold him accountable for setting positive goals that fit the criteria for a well-formed outcome. She will expect him to focus on the mind-body-spirit connection.

Many clients are tempted to dismiss the mind-body-spirit influence as irrelevant. They have reservations about the holistic approach that encourages the client to seek to have balance in his life. Men who quickly appreciate the benefits of having their usual ways of thinking about career choices challenged are reluctant to explore the strategies they use to become self-aware and connect with their spiritual side.

Your spirituality is simply who you are and how you are. In order to connect and communicate with others you need to connect with yourself. It is not enough to have skills. To be an effective communicator you have to understand certain basic facts about yourself as well as about talking and listening.

Words are only a tiny part of communication. So you can be incredibly skilled at using words and fail to get the response you want. You can use brilliant logic, dazzle with your verbal skills and yet fail to communicate the meaning you intend.

Family relationships, teamwork and customer services depend on people being able to communicate. The skills necessary to connect and create rapport can be developed with practise. Please remember that these are skills that all people have naturally in some measure. They more they are used in conscious awareness the more effective they will be.

If you seek to be successful you need to find successful strategies and know why they work. You will need to change what is not working. This means that you will want to be flexible and find new approaches. You will be challenged to move out of your comfort zone and to pay attention to your own experience.

TRUST YOURSELF

In order to fully benefit from the coaching relationship, achieve your desired outcome and become the best that you can be you must have trust – not in your coach but in your own amazing neurological-physiological system. The 'Neuro' part of NLP teaches you that you have choices about what you think and how you feel. It's obvious that when you change what you think you change how you feel. What is not so obvious is that how you think affects your sense of reality.

Let me explain. Your subjective experience includes what goes on inside your mind as well as in the world outside. How you think affects what you achieve and what you fail to achieve. Your thoughts affect your beliefs about the world. Your beliefs have an impact on how successful you are in life.

Your external reality is perceived through your five senses. What you see and hear and smell and taste and touch is your subjective experience. What you perceive as your external world translates into your understanding of what reality is for you. The way you make meaning, understand and experience your world is subjective.

You can have very different responses to what appears to be the same experience. Suppose you place one of your hands in a bowl of hot water and the other in a bowl of cold water. Then you remove your hands and put them both into a bowl of lukewarm water. The hand that was in the hot water will feel cold and the hand that was in the cold water will appear hot.

You respond to your own model of reality and your model of reality is not static. In similar fashion other people respond to their personal models of reality. Once you understand this you can understand why the behaviour and actions of some people don't make any sense to you. They have a different perception of reality. The problem for a man who is out of touch with his feelings and is not self-aware is that he cannot be sensitive to the response of others.

LACK OF AWARENESS

This lack of self-awareness and empathy will have an impact on everyone he meets. If he is part of a team and emotionally bankrupt he is lacking a vital skill. How can he get the best from his staff if he misses the subtle signals that communicate how they respond to or react for or against whatever proposals he puts forward?

So many people who lack self-awareness have the ability and talent to achieve. They can't understand why they fail to reach their goals. Some clients who come for coaching have gone through business failures. They are full of bright ideas for a new venture but they have never given either thought or time to work out what part they played in the failure of the old venture.

It's as though that past failure is buried and all the trauma that went with it is buried too. If you truly want to succeed you need to learn from the mistakes of the past. You need to think about success and failure in a new way. Success means achieving each step on the way to your desired outcome.

I want you to redefine failure and think about it in a new way. Instead of seeing 'Failure' as a negative let's redefine it and find a positive way to view it now. What if we were to think about it as a learning experience that shows us that something done this way does not work? Wouldn't that change a negative into a positive?

What if we were to appreciate the positive benefits of what we used to call 'Failure' and recognise the motivation to be creative and find a different strategy? Wouldn't that help to change what you think and how you feel?

SENSORY AWARENESS

It's not enough to have a specific goal. People who achieve their goals make images in their minds of what they will see and hear and feel when they have their desired outcome. When you think of reaching your goals you need to conjure up bright, colourful, life-size pictures in your mind? You have to be clear about when, where and with whom do you want this. You need to have a sense of what you will see, hear and feel on the inside.

When you tell me that you want to be successful and you paint a vivid a picture of what you will see and how you will feel I catch your enthusiasm. That helps me to feel good about the detailed level of your planning. Your plans give me confidence in your ability to go out and achieve your goals.

If a client tells me that his desired outcome is that he wants to be successful I want to believe he is highly motivated. I want his excitement to be palpable so that I have a sense of how real the whole thing is for him. His belief in his dream is a vital ingredient for success.

Even if a client has worked out all the practical matters, obviously thought them through, has a brilliant planned time frame for completion and he is out of touch with how this makes him feel I will invite him to go back to the drawing board. There is something crucially important missing. The motivation to succeed is powerfully influenced by the belief that he can bring his dream to fruition. If a client is not excited about the end result I want to know why.

When you challenge yourself to enjoy a foretaste of how you feel about achieving your goals it brings your dreams to life. That mental representation will increase your commitment, your motivation to achieve. It will also make for greater satisfaction when you achieve the desired results.

It is only when a client has a mental representation of his outcome that makes him excited about his plans and how he will achieve them that I believe in his will to succeed. If he convinces me that he believes in himself and his outcome he will find successful strategies and he will achieve his goals.

SUMMARY

- How do you motivate yourself?
- Make yourself happy – change what you think.
- You respond to your own model of reality.
- Appreciate the positive benefits of 'Failure.'

'If I had eight hours to cut down a tree, I would spend the first six sharpening the saw'.

ABRAHAM LINCOLN.

CHAPTER 10

SELF SABOTAGE

IN THIS CHAPTER:

- **Fear keeps you stuck.**
- **Emotional honesty requires self-awareness.**
- **Fear of success is as damaging as fear of failure.**

A hotel owner complained bitterly about the effect on his business of a new motorway the Government had built.

'I don't know what you are complaining about,' said a friend. 'I don't understand you. I see a 'No Vacancy' sign each night in front of the hotel.'

'You can't go by that. Before they built the new road I used to turn away thirty or forty people each day. Now I never turn away more than twenty.'

'When you are determined to feel bad,' said his friend, 'You will find reasons to upset yourself.'

WHAT MOTIVATES YOU?

Do you know what the two strongest motivations for all your behaviours are? You want to experience pleasure and avoid pain. The desire for pleasure is reflected in your efforts to get what you think you want. Your attempts to gain personal benefits, like wealth, power, control, approval, or love, unconsciously motivate every desire you have. Those desires are behind everything you do.

The desire to avoid pain, discomfort, criticism, hassle, poverty or loss of your job is the motivation behind much of what you do or fail to do. You may not recognise this but avoiding discomfort is the powerful motivator behind most of the things that you do under duress. And what you will find when you sit quietly and check what is going on inside you is that there is fear and sometimes anger in you.

Anything you do because you believe you have to do it is born out of some level of fear. Fear is at the root of feeling stuck. Behind almost every reason a person has for failing to achieve you will find it lurking in many different guises. Think about it for a moment. What stops you from taking risks? For what purpose do you avoid doing what at some level you want to do? The bottom line is fear in some guise. It may be fear of the consequences, fear of failure, fear of success, fear of the unknown or a combination of all of these.

When you know something is wrong and you tell yourself that you should do something but don't, look for what stops you. Stress, worry, anxiety, nervousness, tension are just other names for one of the most powerful de-motivating emotions - fear.

When you have worked really hard, when you complain that your work is not valued but do not ask for what you believe you deserve, what gets in the way? Clients will always have a reason and when their coach challenges their rationale, guess what she will find? Nine times out of ten the client is motivated by some kind of fear that prevents him making changes.

It's understandable if you find it difficult to become self-motivated and risk working on your own initiative. It's hard to solve a problem where you're dealing with hidden fear. It doesn't really matter if what you fear is real or exists only in your imagination. The effect is similar. Once fear is in you it gets in the way of achievement. It limits your options and prevents you from reaching your potential.

The fear of criticism is a very common fear. It causes discomfort and upset feelings in many people. In almost every situation where one person is critical of another there is a communication problem. The criticiser wants something from the other that he is not getting. He may be seeking something that will be of benefit to the other person but that is not what is communicated. What is perceived as humour by one person can be interpreted as bullying by another.

Poor communication is at the core of many interpersonal difficulties. In many instances a client discovers that he is so sensitive to criticism that he picks it up where it was not intended. Say his boss comments on a report he has written and says, 'This is not what I expected.' How he interprets that comment will depend on his own expectations of how he has done. If his self-esteem is high he may believe 'My boss thinks this is better than he expected.' If it's low he will assume that his boss is dissatisfied.

His coach will encourage clients to ask curious questions like, 'What specifically did you expect?' I remember one client who worked for a company that had annual reviews. He believed that his boss was never happy with his reports and dreaded the review.

I asked him did he have evidence for his opinion. He knew by how his boss looked. Judging by someone's expressions is not a very accurate way of monitoring how you are doing. Many clients behave as mind readers. They make assumptions about what their boss wants because they fear that they will look bad if they ask questions. When my client learned to ask specific questions and clarify what was expected of him his work situation improved. He had his boss take responsibility for his poor instructions. There was fault on both sides. It was his boss's responsibility to give clearer instructions and my clients to ask questions if the communication was not clear.

WHAT STOPS YOU ACHIEVING?

A coach is fine-tuned to pick up hidden fears and challenge the illogical thinking that appears real to her client. Clients have an amazing capacity for rationalisation. I want to stress that the feeling response in the client is real. It's how he thinks that has to be challenged and changed.

What you think and feel is always real to you but when it is examined it may not stand up to scrutiny. Personal change cannot happen until a client becomes honest with his feelings. Being emotionally honest requires a level of self-awareness and self- acceptance that is often difficult for a client.

There is no denying that hardly anyone is fully aware of the motivation behind the choices he makes. A small number of clients will have done some personal development work and will know exactly what their problem is and how to resolve issues. Others who are less aware will know that there is something wrong without being able to say what exactly is causing their disquiet. You cannot solve a problem until you know what it is.

Few clients ever consider the secondary gain that is closely aligned with self-sabotage. A surprising number of clients are frustrated and dissatisfied. They cannot explain why or understand how they find themselves in that position. Usually when they work with a coach they find that they are part of the problem.

It's surprising how often people are their own worst enemy. They turn up late for an interview, they swear at their boss, they lose an important report. Of course they say it was an accident or bad luck. Your coach will encourage you to move beyond making excuses and ask you to take responsibility. Clients have a part to play when something is done badly.

You will make your own luck when you realise that there is no problem that does not have a solution. Always have a fallback strategy. Once you see a problem as an opportunity it's possible to set about finding creative solutions.

SELF-SABOTAGE

A very common reason why people fail to live up to their potential is they are afraid of failure. Low achievers can rationalise failure to themselves in very articulate and well thought out ways but the truth is they will not move out of their comfort zone. The risk of failure is too worrying so they never really give themselves a chance to shine.

It is not so widely recognised that people also fear success. Many highly intelligent adults value resources and strengths in others that they possess but do not recognise in themselves. They have a distorted way of thinking, a sort of false modesty that makes them afraid to achieve their potential.

Many clients are amazed to discover that they fear success. Until they are challenged to say what stops them achieving they fail to recognise how they are their own worst enemy. I had one client who was a brilliant negotiator. He comes from a dysfunctional family. Both his parents were alcoholics and his father was violent.

He believed that what stopped him being more successful in life was cowardice. He put the label of coward on himself and lived up to it in his own estimation. It wasn't hard to find where the fear came from because he lived in fear as a child.

The powerful revelation when he did the 'How am I?' exercise was the discovery that he had an enormous amount of courage. As a twelve years old boy he often had to physically separate his father and mother. 'How did you do that?' I asked. 'I was a skilled manipulator. I did anything. I begged, pleaded, cajoled, whatever I had to do to get them off each other.' 'I had courage   At times I was risking life and limb.' What a life-changing insight for that man.

Blame springs from fear and is nurtured by the belief that one is helpless. When people who work with a coach are reluctant to take responsibility for what they do and how they feel she looks for fear. The client may blame other people or lack of educational qualifications or life situations for stopping him from getting ahead. The coach will challenge her client to test the validity of every explanation he gives. In the process he will be challenged to get in touch with the feelings that he is denying or trying to ignore. In this process he will gain insights into how his own beliefs stop him. Such insights happen in an instant and they are really life changing.

COACHING CARL

When I work with clients I expect them to be willing to be emotionally honest. In order to learn to think in a new way a client has to be willing to think the unfamiliar. He has to learn how to be honest with himself. He also wants to have realistic expectations and not set out to achieve everything all at once. When the client accepts that he is his own most important resource and his own worst enemy he has choices. He can acknowledge the strategies he uses to stop himself achieving his stated goals. Then he can look for new, more successful ones.

So many clients channel their energies in negative and destructive ways. They waste energy by worrying and fretting and believe that this is normal behaviour. So often a client challenges me by asking, 'Doesn't everyone worry?' Rather than give an answer I let the client discover that he has the answer in himself.

The role of a coach is to assist the client in finding his own answers. One small insight can influence how he thinks and feels about many other areas. Let's say I am working with a client who is a chronic worrier. He is not aware of it but there is a secondary gain, a benefit that he gets from worrying. I could explain the theory of positive intention to him. He wouldn't have a problem understanding and agreeing with my explanation at a head level. To recognise the logic is not enough. The client needs to have an experience of how understanding changes perceptions.

Explaining the theory to the client is not as effective a way of working as empowering the client to discover this for himself. Once he recognises that there is a negative payoff that is not helpful he is half-way to finding the solution that will work for him. The client is in the best position to find a positive way to move forward. The coach will ask the right questions to encourage his progress.

Carl	Doesn't everyone worry?
Coach	I'm not sure that everyone does. I've a curious question for you.
	Ask yourself, 'Is it logical to upset yourself about something that may never happen? Is it logical to feel distressed because you make an assumption about what you believe someone else is thinking?'
Carl	What do you mean?
Coach	You remember how worried you were about applying for leave for your sister's wedding. You said that your boss probably wouldn't sanction it and you were very

concerned that you might have to take sick leave. However if you did that and your boss found out you would have no excuse. You had yourself sick with worry for days before you applied.

Think about what you did to yourself for those few days. Your upset was real and it was your response to what you were telling yourself. What do you think motivated you to do that to yourself?

Carl	I suppose it's habit. All of my family are worriers.
Coach	What do you get, what is the benefit you derive from worry?
Carl	I never thought of it like that before. I can't think of anything that I gain from worrying.
Coach	Think about it. At a logical level you say you don't gain anything from worrying. I accept that is your belief. However I want you to think, really think, about what hidden benefit you get?
Carl	It's familiar. It's kind of a way that I deal with things. I'm used to having that kind of knotted feeling in my stomach. I never realised that all that tension is of my own making. I put myself through that and didn't realise what I was doing.
Coach	What a useful insight. Now that you understand what you do to yourself when you worry you can have other choices. Will that make a difference to you?
Carl	Yes.

'THE GREMLIN'

When there is hassle in your life, where does it come from? You may begin to answer this question by looking outside yourself and blaming your boss or your partner or your financial situation for creating the upset. One or all of these can stimulate massive stress or upset BUT it is not the situation or event that is responsible for how you feel. It's your own thinking that produces those feeling.

If you are the client an effective coach will encourage you to take responsibility for what you feel. When you do and you go back to explore what you are feeling and what you are thinking, guess what you will find? – The negative little voice inside your head. Whether you are aware of it or not you talk to yourself. Like many other coaches I nickname this part of clients their 'Gremlin.'

Many people fail to achieve their goals because they talk to themselves in a negative way. They have preconceived ideas based on bad experiences of the past and they seem to be unable to overcome those experiences. It's like they are in a time warp. They generalise from one experience when they failed and sabotage their own efforts with negativity that was bred in childhood. We will call that inner self-sabotaging voice 'The Gremlin.'

How would you know if you have 'The Gremlin?' How would you know if you have a part of you that sabotages your efforts? Here are a few pointers. Many of the rationalisations you make to explain why you fail to do what you commit to do can be traced to 'The Gremlin.' Many of the fears that get in the way of your taking risks come from the same source.

One of the reasons why I keep telling clients how important it is to grow in self-awareness is that I want them to have a clear understanding of their own reasons and motivation. Awareness will give insights that can bring instant change when the client becomes aware of a positive choice and he opts for this. It is so simple for a client to discover the benefits of understanding his own motivation. I cannot emphasise enough how important it is to be aware of the purpose for which you do things.

Clients are often surprised when I ask them to befriend 'The Gremlin.' 'Why would you want to show gratitude to the self sabotaging part of yourself?' is one of the usual questions I'm asked. 'Because the behaviour that you now want to eliminate originated at one time in your life to meet a genuine need you had. That behaviour once served you well. It may be useful to you again in the future. You don't want to get rid of it. You just want to find a more appropriate strategy for the issues you are dealing with at this point in your life.'

One of the theories in NLP is that behind everything a person says or does there is a positive intention that makes perfect sense to the person. He or she will have a positive motive that may be very well hidden. Through the personal interaction in a coaching session the layers of negativity can be peeled away and the underlying positive intention discovered. The motive is always for some good for the client. His behaviour in getting what he wants may be childish and totally inappropriate.

EXERCISE: AM I STRONG OR WEAK?

Are you aware that you when you think in a positive way your body is strong? When you think in a negative way the energy flow in your body is disrupted and your body weakens. Just try out a simple little exercise with a friend to demonstrate that this is true.

Get your friend to hold out his arm parallel to the floor.
Push gently on his wrist in order to test how far it moves down towards the floor.
Now get your friend to repeat 'I'm weak, I'm weak, I'm weak' as you gently tap his wrist.

Count and after he has repeated it about ten times push the wrist towards the floor and watch what happens.

The arm will be weak and move downwards towards the floor. In some people it will literally collapse and drop down to the person's side. Get the friend to put his arm up again. This time tap the wrist while he says 'I'm strong, I'm strong, I'm strong.'

After he repeats this nine or ten times push the arm towards the floor. It will be even stronger than when you started the exercise. It won't budge. Get him to continue repeating the phrase. The more he repeats 'I'm strong' the stronger his arm will become.

You will get the same results from using other negative statements and changing them into positive ones. 'I'm a bad boy' weakens the arm. 'I'm a good boy' strengthens it. 'I hate maths' weakens the body. The fascinating thing about these exercises is that when a person states what he wants in positive terms even when it is not yet true for him his body remains strong. Change to 'I love maths' and the arm will be stronger.

If you ever find yourself neglecting you own needs and feeling murderously resentful of people who dump on you it's time you got to know 'The Gremlin.' Perhaps you are co-responsible for what is happening. I'm not denying that some people are selfish and take advantage of others.

We all know people who believe in looking after 'Number one' and are ruthless with anyone who objects. We also know people who play weak. They refuse to take responsibility in an adult way. There are people who bring their problems and difficulties and dump them on others. For every person who plays helpless and gets away with it there is a willing carer to play the role of rescuer.

Issues to do with personal responsibility need to be addressed in most coaching relationships. The coach has only to skim the surface of any issue on the client's agenda and underneath she will find longstanding attitudes and beliefs that block logical thinking and prevent good self-care.

You don't have to be an Einstein to recognise that self-esteem issues are closely tied to the workings of 'The Gremlin.' As a tiny child you were trained to ask permission from adults for almost everything you did. You were told where to hang your coat and how to rule your copybook and your mother probably even decided how much food you should eat. That was necessary when you were a child. Internal rules that have you constantly checking things are outdated and are certainly limiting for an adult. When you question yourself and ask, 'Is this how I should do this?' you give control to others.

Your intention when you ask, 'Do you mind if I do something' may be to be polite. That's a healthy reason but learn to be aware of the times when you ask permission because you are not willing to take responsibility. So many people give away their personal power without being aware of how this limits their choices.

How can you possibly achieve your full potential if you make the opinion of others more important than your own? If you hesitate about making decisions that you know you are competent to make you are giving away your power. Any time you tell yourself 'I should,' 'I must,' 'I ought,' or 'I have to,' you do the same. If you use one of those words it is necessary to STOP and ask 'Why should I? Change to 'I want to' or 'I choose to' or 'I don't want to' and you are in control. It's your choice to do whatever it is.

Reflect on the effect of the message that you are giving to yourself. As a grown-up you want to make free choices about what you say and do. If you are programmed to check things out mentally you are giving 'The Gremlin' immense power. Self-sabotage is common and so widely accepted that it is rarely recognised for the damaging force that it is. Instead of saying 'I ought to' and 'I have to,' change and say 'I want' or 'I choose' and you give yourself a choice that empowers you.

Your programmed thinking comes from parents, teachers, youth leaders and others who had authority over you in childhood. Simply ask yourself 'Do I want to?' or 'Is this something I would choose to do?' and your own authentic voice will come through.

You know that stating a goal in negative language will give the wrong message to your brain. This is because the unconscious mind does not recognise negative words. Young children seem to know this instinctively. Watch even very young children playing games and you will see what I mean.

Without being aware of it they use that intuitive knowledge to win an advantage over a rival when playing games. When you hear a young lad shout at his opponent 'Don't miss the ball,' you can anticipate what will happen. The opponent will probably miss. Why? Because the unconscious mind ignores the work 'Don't. The message it responds to is 'Miss the ball.' His intention is to distract in order to put the other player off his game.

The widespread assumption is that it is the shouted command that breaks the opponents concentration. The more accurate explanation is that the phrase has an implication that what is suggested will definitely happen and it does. When I tell you that 'You don't have to take my word for this' you will most likely have a predictable response. At the surface level that statement is true. You can't argue with it, but under the surface is what is called an embedded command. You don't have to understand how this works for it to work.

SUMMARY

- Discovering how negative pay-offs work.
- Meeting 'The Gremlin.'
- Don't give your personal power away.

'What has been believed by all always and everywhere has every likelihood of being untrue'.

PAUL VALERY.

CHAPTER 11

EMPOWERING CHOICES

IN THIS CHAPTER:

- **Keep your personal power.**
- **New insights change you.**
- **Drop unrealistic expectations.**
- **Be wary of your beliefs.**
- **You always have choices.**

A Spiritual Master taught that one reason that people are so unhappy is that they think there is nothing that they cannot change.
He especially enjoyed the story of the man who said to the shop owner. This sound system you sold me is excellent for quality. But I want to exchange the radio for one that has better programmes.

ITS NOT THE SITUATION YOU ARE IN BUT YOUR THINKING THAT MAKES IT FEEL GOOD OR BAD

Your values have a powerful impact on what you believe you can and cannot do. When you believe you have a choice you are in charge of your own actions. You feel empowered.

Every day you make decisions to do or not do different things. You are not even aware you have made many of these choices. Positive choices empower you. Negative choices are disempowering. You give away your personal power when you tell yourself that you don't have a choice. You have 'Blinkered vision' when you limit your options. Reframing 'I can't' to 'I can't yet' gives two very different messages to the brain.

The choices you make during the day regardless of how trivial they may seem to you contribute to making you feel satisfied or dissatisfied with your life. Every decision you make whether you are aware of it or not moves you towards or away from balance in your life.

I suspect that if I asked you 'Would you allow yourself to be treated like a robot that is powered by remote control?' you would say 'No.' If I suggested that most of us act in a robotic way you would probably deny that this is true. Yet any time you do something because you believe you 'Should,' 'Must,' 'Ought' or 'Have to' you are not in charge of your own actions. You are allowing your actions to be controlled by the expectations you believe others have of you. If your life is not controlled by your own choices you have given your personal power away, haven't you?

If you answer 'Yes' to any of the following questions you are being influenced and controlled externally. In the measure that you are dependent on the approval of others you give them the remote control of your life. They push your buttons and you respond.

Do you ever find that you are:
- devastated by criticism?
- worried about upsetting your spouse or partner?
- fearful about challenging a colleague?
- anxious in case you meet with disapproval?
- afraid to speak out about a perceived injustice?
- frustrated by what others expect of you?

If you answer 'Yes' to any of these question you may be allowing yourself to be controlled by externals. The tragedy is that you are not yet aware that you are giving control over your life away. You have not yet discovered that you make the opinion and presence of others more important than your own. They hold the remote control of your life. They press the disapproval button and you are devastated. They press flattery and you are delighted.

When you are devastated by criticism you are putting the demands and opinions of others above your own wants. If you respect your right to think your own thoughts and you give equal respect to the rights of other people to think in any way they choose then criticism will not hurt you. Your opinion is right for you. The other person's is right for them.

The hurt comes when you make their opinion more important than yours. When you exalt them and what they think you put yourself down. If you are hurt by criticism you are blaming the other for putting you down. You have accepted their criticism. How would your response to criticism be different if you were to tell yourself 'My perception is valid for me. Other peoples' perceptions are valid for them.'

It would change everything, wouldn't it? You are now dealing with a difference of opinion. When I work with clients I invite them to go one step further. Usually when one person is critical of another they want something that they are not getting from that person. It's remarkable how a client moves from feeling disempowered when he recognises the part his thinking plays in the process. Once he gets this empowering insight he has the tools to see things in a new way.

Your goal in life is not to live up to the expectations of others or to the unconscious expectations you have of yourself. As your Life Coach I want you to expand your thinking and to wake up and understand that you have the power to change what you think. When you have new insights you change how you feel.

You now understand that when you allow yourself to be devastated by criticism you are telling yourself that other people's opinions are more important than your own. You are hurting yourself. Your feelings are your response to what you think and how you make meaning.

Now I want you to go through any questions to which you answered yes in order to reflect on what you are telling yourself. Don't judge yourself. You now have the tools to understand yourself better.

EXERCISE: HOW IMPORTANT IS MY OPINION?

Be creative when you do the following exercise. Use your imagination. Brainstorm and use humour to understand what you are thinking. These insights have the potential to be life changing.

When you are worried about upsetting your spouse or partner how are you making her opinion more important than yours?

_____

_____

_____

When you are fearful about challenging a colleague how are you making his opinion more important than yours?

_____

_____

_____

When you are anxious in case you meet with disapproval how are you making someone else's opinion more important than yours?

_____

_____

_____

When you are afraid to speak out about a perceived injustice how are you making someone else's opinion more important than yours?

_____

_____

_____

When you are frustrated by what others expect of you how are you making their opinion more important than yours?

_____

_____

_____

When you change your thinking, YOU change.

LOOK AT ALL YOUR OPTIONS

People feel stuck in impossible situations because they tell themselves they have no choices. They box themselves in. They limit their choices by trying to live up to expectations, their own and those of others. Often they blame others for putting them under pressure when the problem is really their own unrealistic expectations.

Once you learn how to look and broaden your vision by seeing other possible explanations you will discover that a whole new vista opens up. Let me give you an example of how this works. Imagine a person believes that he has to do work he doesn't enjoy for whatever reasons. Perhaps he has to pay the mortgage, or he doesn't want to lose the status his job brings, or he wants to keep the company car. He believes he is stuck in the situation and while he holds onto that belief he is right.

What you believe is true becomes true for you. If you believe you have no choice you are stuck. If you tell yourself that there is no way out you are unlikely to search for other options. Be wary of your beliefs. They can easily become self-fulfilling prophesies. While it is important to be aware of how you are thinking there are many other disempowering factors that must be taken into consideration. Negative thinking has a powerful influence on the belief system of a person who feels he has limited choices.

YOU ALWAYS HAVE CHOICES

Anything you do that is not your free choice takes away your personal power. Say Brendan tells his Life Coach that he wants to exercise but can't. He has a good reason. The coach will listen to his rationalisation and make sure that Brendan feels heard before she offers any challenges to the veracity of what is said.

The conversation could go something like this.

Brendan   I really want to exercise but I'm so busy at work that I can't.

Coach	Sounds like you are really busy. I'm hearing that you really want to exercise and that you feel this is impossible because of your workload. Is there a way you could make time to do any kind of exercise?
Brendan	I have a project coming up and I have to put in a lot of overtime for the next two weeks. I just can't take on anything else.
Coach	How do you like to exercise?
Brendan	I like to go to the gym and have a good workout and a steam.
Coach	Seems like you can't make time for the gym for the next couple of weeks. However I think you might find it useful to explore alternative ways of incorporating exercise into your busy schedule. Can you think of any ways you might do this going to or coming from work?
Brendan	I suppose I could leave my car at home. I have thought about it but with the bus lanes I would probably travel quicker than in the car. I could get off a few stops away and walk part of the way.
Coach	So walking is an option. Can you think of anything else you might do?
Brendan	I could walk upstairs instead of taking the lift. I could do stretching exercises at my desk.
Coach	Sounds like you can enjoy exercises without the treadmill and stepper in the gym.

DISCOVERING YOUR OPTIONS

I cannot repeat often enough that in every situation you have choices. You decide how to make meaning of what you see and your emotional response comes from what you choose to think. Let me give you a wonderful example of what is known as interpretive looking.

Two council employees were hard at work on the road in front of a house of ill repute when they saw a rabbi slink into the brothel. 'Well, what can you expect?' they said to each other. After a while a vicar slipped in. No surprise. 'What can you expect?' Then came their local Catholic priest who wore his hat low to cover his face just before he slipped into the building. 'Now isn't that terrible? One of those unfortunate girls must have taken ill.'

When your self-sabotaging little voice uses words like 'Can't' it's deceiving you. It wants you to believe that 'As it was in the beginning, is now and ever shall be.' Statements like, 'I can't do it,' 'I'm not able,' 'I was never good at it' are red flag signals that you are stuck in old thinking. 'Can't' shuts the door on change.

A tiny addition to the sentence will open the door to new possibilities. Simply add the little word 'yet.' 'I can't do it yet' signals the possibility that if I make an effort, reorganise my time, have a shorter lunch break, get up earlier, use public transport or whatever I choose to do, I will be successful. When I really want to exercise I will find the time even if it means dropping something else.

Clients who have no intention of lying tell a story they believe. They give explanations that make perfect sense to them. When the coach asks the right questions clients find that their explanation of how things are does not stand up to scrutiny. They are rationalising.

The client does not intend to lie or deceive. His vision is limited to an 'Either/or' scenario. Once he sees it in a different way his view is expanded. His perception is challenged. He can take other options into consideration. Choices become clearer and numerous options can be found for situations that at one time appeared to have no solution.

THE SAME ACTION CAN BE EMPOWERING OR DISEMPOWERING.

Ten different people can do exactly the same job and they will have ten different beliefs about how satisfying they find the work. It's not the work. It's the way people think about the work that creates a positive or negative attitude towards the job.

Let me make it even simpler. The person's attitude is what determines whether a task is satisfying or boring, empowering or soul destroying. One person can do something as basic as cook a meal. Whether that action is an empowering or disempowering action will depend on the person and how he thinks about the task.

If you make a meal because you believe you have to cook, you are disempowered by your own belief. You are controlled from outside, by the belief that 'You have to.' When you engage in the same act of cooking because you choose to make the meal the control is internal. You are empowered when it's your choice. You disempower yourself when the control is external. The difference is a very subtle and important one and it has a huge impact on how you experience life.

When you give control of your life away you feel disempowered. Another way of looking at this is any time you find that you are living up to the expectations of others you are not in charge of your own life. This is true whether the control is exercised by a person standing over you and telling you what you should do or by your own expectations of what they expect from you. It's amazing how learning about choices help you feel in control. It teaches you to understand how you empower or dis-empower yourself by the choices you make.

When you become self-aware your life changes for the better. When you understand how you think and why you are responding the way you do you can make different choices. Remember you are in control of how you think and what you do. You will be amazed at how good you feel when you tell yourself 'I want to do this' rather than 'I have to' or 'I should.'

STUCK IN A RUT?

In every situation in life a person has many options that he fails to recognise as choices. Let's say Alan gets a Life Coach because he hates his job. He has financial commitments to meet so for the foreseeable future he believes he is stuck in a rut. One aspect of Alan's problem is that he genuinely believes he has no options.

We both know that this is only his perception. It is not his reality because in every situation he has many choices. When he goes to work to earn money even though he says he hates his job, Alan is making a choice. He could make many other choices and each one would have a different consequence.

He could give up the job but he is not prepared to live with the consequence of doing so. That is also a choice. Another option is he could get Social Security but that would mean he is not in a position to take care of his financial commitments. He could look for another job, ask for a transfer within the company or seek a promotion. Each option has a consequence.

Another interesting choice that Alan may not think about is that he could explore what it is about his job that causes such strong negative feelings. 'I hate my job' is a generalisation. Setting out to discover what it is specifically about the job that he hates could be a most enlightening experience.

Once Alan understands that the rut he is in is of his own making he can begin to plan how he can get out of that rut. A hugely important part of the coaching process is learning about choices. Let's say that he makes a decision to continue in his current job because he needs the money. He thinks about it now in a different way. Instead of believing that he has no choice he now tells himself that he is deciding to work here.

This is now a positive empowering choice. The work won't change but Alan's attitude to it will change radically for the better. Once he explores all his options and makes the decision to continue in the job something really important happens in Alan. He no longer feels trapped and disempowered although whatever he disliked about the job remains the same.

What is different is that he will now be going to work because he has freely made this choice. His changed attitude will affect how he feels. The trapped feelings that were a constant irritant when he felt he had no choice, when he felt disempowered, go away. The benefit to Alan is that he now understands that he can make a choice to continue doing what he dislikes and survive. This moves him from being stuck to having a sense of control and you can see how helpful this insight will be when he is planning for his future. By learning what specifically he dislikes about the job and what resources he has to help him stay with it he has a lot of useful information that will help him plan for his future.

He will be a better employee. It is even possible that his change of mind, moving from 'I have to' to 'I choose to' will help him enjoy aspects of work that he once hated. I've known a few clients who believe that their change of attitude helped them get a promotion.

THERE IS MORE THAN ONE WAY TO SKIN A RABBIT

When you believe you have no choice in a situation you feel trapped. When you learn how many different choices you have you gain a certain freedom that makes the process of clarifying your goals more interesting.

There is an old saying that 'There is more than one way to skin a rabbit.' You now understand that in every situation in your life you have many different options that you can allow yourself the freedom to explore. You do not make isolated choices in one area of your life. When you change in one area other areas are affected by the change.

When you work with a coach you are challenged to expand your horizon, to think in new ways. She will listen to what you say and pick up on what is not said and on what she perceives you may be avoiding. She will get you to question every choice you consider and get you to examine the beliefs you have that will impact on different areas of your life.

When you accept the consequences of the life choices you make you feel more motivated to go after your goals. When you are encouraged to recognise that you have the skills and strengths to get what you want you feel more in control. Your coach will hold you responsible for fully exploring all the consequences of achieving the outcome you desire. She will highlight incongruity and challenge rationalisations through reflective questioning.

You will be surprised at how big a difference working with someone who feels confident that you can succeed will make to your motivation. It is so encouraging to feel understood by a coach who believes in you 100% and who holds you accountable for unlocking your potential to achieve.

SUMMARY

- **The magic word 'Yet.'**
- **There is always a solution.**
- **You empower or dis-empower yourself.**
- **Your perception is not reality.**
- **You always have choices.**

'Learn to work harder on yourself than you do on your job. If you work hard on your job you will earn a living. If you work hard on yourself you will make a fortune'.

JIM ROHN.

CHAPTER 12

EXECUTIVE COACHING

IN THIS CHAPTER:

- Different styles of executive coaching.

- Failure to listen costs money and goodwill.

- Build on strengths and identify weakness.

A business executive asked what was the secret of successful living?
Said the guru 'make one person happy each day.'
As an afterthought he added 'even if that person is yourself.'
A minute passed and he said 'especially if that person is yourself.'

DIFFERENT STYLES OF EXECUTIVE COACHING

The aim of coaching is similar to that of successful management –
to achieve profitable growth. Peter Bolt author of 'The Whole
Manager' says 'If more organisations developed coaching as a key
element of their management strategy or approach then there
would be more thriving, highly effective and well motivated teams
in organisations of all kinds.'

The term Executive Coaching is ambiguous because it may refer to
an outside coach working with chief executives and senior
managers in a one-to-one capacity, or it may refer to in-house
coaching where individual staff members are coached by senior
management either as individuals or as part of a group. It may also
come as part of a package deal. Some trainers offer complimentary
Executive Coaching to the person who has responsibility for
implementing changes after staff training.

One-to-one Executive Coaching presents a challenge to the coach because high achievers who have top jobs are typically accomplished and confident people, at least on the outside. They are used to stating views that staff do not question. It can be intimidating for a coach when it is necessary to challenge the boss about issues that create problems for his staff.

Most companies are pleasantly surprised by the positive changes in the working environment when staff members work with a coach. An organisation's most valuable resource is its staff and effective coaching has a very positive impact on performance at all levels. Individuals and the organisation benefit when there is honest evaluation and people are developed to their full potential.

REALISTIC EVALUATION

In many organisations managers believe that they are doing an excellent job. At the end of the day they feel good about what they have achieved. While it is wonderful that any manager is happy at his job and feels good about his work that is not the evidence that the coach seeks to convince her that he is an effective manager.

She will be looking for more concrete evidence of his achievements. She will want him to be clear about what exactly is better and how objectively the improvements are measured. Working with a coach each manager is invited to be specific about his job responsibilities, what he does and what he hopes to achieve. She will want him to be able to set realistic goals for improvements that are owned by him. The clarity about work practices that comes from this exercise can make a big difference in output, production and sales.

The skilled Executive Coach needs to be decisive and have the courage of her convictions. Executives are often protected from the impact they have on staff down the scale. The boss who creates an atmosphere where mistakes are hidden and nobody wants to take a risk needs to be made aware that failure to hear what the people on the ground have to say will cost the company goodwill and money.

DEALING WITH CHANGE

The first challenge for a company that is dealing with change is to get employees to know and clearly understand what is happening and why. Companies that have problems with trade unions when implementing change pay a high price. So many issues can be resolved if managers take time to listen to staff. Without the commitment of everyone in the organisation the best strategy in the world will fail. It is not difficult to see the signs of a failed strategy. Ask staff what they think about changes that are proposed. If you hear things like, 'It's not possible,' or 'The change is not worth the inconvenience,' your implementation strategy is not working.

The coach will encourage executives to involve staff early and tell them as much as possible. Bosses are often too remote and fail to listen to opinions and suggestions from the people who are expected to deal with cost cutting strategies or market new products or implement whatever initiatives are currently on the drawing board. Enormous damage is done by executives and consultants when they fail to communicate their strategies for change. Many executives who believe that they are acting in a decisive manner are regarded as bullies by their co-workers.

The best way to bring employees on board is to have a strategy for communicating the business benefits and what is in it for the employees. A direct conversation between team leaders, managers or supervisors works well. Get staff involved and have the people who do the work involved in redesigning procedures that have to be changed. Explain how it is planned to make sure that staff has the knowledge, skills and support to make the new strategy work. Be clear about the plans to provide training and ongoing coaching.

BULLYING

It is easier and safer for a person outside the organisation to challenge insidious bullying. There is no denying that a lot of bullying takes places in the workplace. A client of mine who is a manager complained that her boss believed he had a great relationship with his staff. When I asked, 'What makes him think this?' she acknowledged that she was intimidated by him as were her co-workers. They were afraid to challenge him so she acknowledged that she had a part to play in giving her boss grounds for his wrong beliefs.

Normally an outgoing and talkative person it was hard for my client to admit that she became tongue-tied with this man. With other colleagues she expressed her opinions openly. She was very disappointed with herself and came to me because she was so upset that she didn't seem to be able to stand up to him.

She recounted an experience in the recent past when he had sent for her. When she went to his office he didn't even invite her to sit down. She was furious as she stood in front of his desk and he informed her of drastic changes in the IT department. She stood silently and said not a single word.

She had information that he didn't have. She knew that if she told him he would change the decision he proposed to make. She wasn't sure if she stayed quiet because she didn't have the courage to speak out or whether she was so angry that she deliberately kept silent knowing that he would have to take the overall responsibility for the debacle that would follow the changes in the department.

This woman got the job because she was self-motivated, ambitious, forward thinking and a self-starter. She performed well and was devastated that she could feel bullied. She was so intimidated by her boss that in front of him she turned to jelly and could not speak up for herself.

This client became passive and non-assertive with a boss who deluded himself about what a good relationship he had with his staff. She fed his belief by her failure to give feedback or be assertive. Underneath the presenting issues the client brought to coaching were her own unhealthy beliefs. She told herself that she was powerless to do anything to change the situation if she wanted to stay in that job. In this instance both the manager and her boss had issues that could be resolved in coaching.

As we continued to work together she grew in self-awareness and made some fascinating discoveries. She believed that she was a great manager because her staff told her what a good job she was doing. When I challenged her to find evidence she realised that she also was intimidated by her staff but in a different way. She discovered that she avoided conflict and was more lenient than she realised.

When we worked on communication skills she found techniques to help her talk with staff about improving their performance. Two suggestions that she found incredibly helpful were to drop using the word 'But' and substitute 'And,' and to sandwich a negative comment between two positive comments about what was going well.

This was not an easy adaptation for her. It often took effort on her part to stop and think about what was going well. A remarkable benefit she found was that she began to watch out for increased productivity. Staff felt affirmed and job performance and job satisfaction increased for everyone.

Executive Coaching is similar to Life Coaching in ways that I have already explained. The focus will usually be on skills and competencies. The client's presenting issue will be dealt with in a context. The coach will help the client decide on the six or eight most important areas that impact on his work and environment. They become the basis of the exercises for a well-formed outcome. So instead of career, money, health, friends and family etc. you could include results, strategic planning, customer services, team development or whatever headings you find useful.

COMMUNICATION

Communication is an essential skill that is rarely valued highly enough. It involves the giving and receiving of information. It is the foundation of team building and customer services. Whenever there is conflict or bullying in an organisation there are communication difficulties. Managers are described as 'Tough but fair,' 'Soft,' or the most sensitive of all 'A bully.'

A bully is a person who uses strength or influence to intimidate or harm others who are weaker. Bullying is an emotive issue because it involves the behaviour of one person and the perception of someone else. In the same organisation some employees feel they are being bullied by a boss and others with the same boss see no problem. The boss truthfully claims that he treats everyone in the same manner and can't understand why people react in such different ways.

A coach can quickly enlighten him. Effective communicators gain rapport by understanding how to match language and non-verbal behaviour. It doesn't matter what contentious issue creates upset or in what context. The root cause of the problem is always communication and it can usually be resolved.

People feel upset and become angry when they don't feel heard. When an executive or manager understands how to communicate effectively he has the tools to close any negotiations in a positive way. The same techniques will prove useful for an executive who is closing a deal with trade unions or his most valued client.

Personalised one-to-one coaching focuses on a person's strengths and his perceived weaknesses. Understanding how you talk to yourself, how you build self-esteem and eliminate negative self-talk is as important for executives and managers as it is for clerks.

When negotiating the sale of an expensive item or agreeing a long term contract for a service industry the relationship between the executive and buyer will last for weeks or months or longer. In the early stages of doing business rapport is high. If unexpected difficulties come up before the contract is signed rapport can be lost very quickly.

It is essential for an executive to have the communication skills to read the situation accurately. If he is not sensitive to the level of rapport how can he detect when it is lost? Many sales are lost because an insensitive boss has never developed the skills to rebuild rapport quickly and save the situation.

Research has shown that 83% of all sales are based on the customer liking the sales person. A customer who is dissatisfied will take his custom elsewhere. Studies also show that an employee who feels liked and appreciated in his job is likely remain with a company even though he could earn more elsewhere. I hardly need to spell out the economic benefits of retaining highly trained and loyal staff.

Communication is an essential skill for anyone who is managing people. Employees need to know exactly what is expected of them in order to meet standards and deliver within agreed timescales. When their efforts to achieve are noticed and commented on people feel valued and appreciated. They respond by giving of their best. Good communication fosters loyalty by appreciation of effort as well as better productivity.

Some firms like to adapt the wheel of life exercise to the needs of their company. If you want to do this for business you can use the template of the wheel at the back of the book. Fill in the titles of the segments that are appropriate to your agenda and follow the instructions. Make an inventory as you did for the wheel of life and score your level of satisfaction. Ideally you will include, family, spirituality and fun and recreation.

INHOUSE COACHING

Coaching usually occurs between an individual and their direct manager or another senior person in the organisation. It is not another form of supervision. It works by making staff more responsible and less dependent on their managers to solve their own problems.

Employees who have been working at the same job for a long time can get complacent. Familiarity can lead to decreased motivation and a loss of clarity about the person's role in the company. Coaching sets clear objectives for the job and helps staff recognise and overcome any barriers to effective performance.

CONFIDENTIALITY

Coaching offers cost-effective personalised development. It involves personalised one-to-one support and focuses on the individual's strengths and weaknesses. The open communication helps to identify problems and makes it easier to make changes. When coaching is introduced into a company, productivity, creativity and communication improves.

Different coaches have different styles of working. It's clear that there must be complete trust between the coach and the client. Each member of staff whatever their level in the organisation must feel free to speak without fear of being judged. Confidentiality and trust are essential. Managers must be aware that no conversation between a client and coach will be repeated.

The job of a coach is not to solve an individual's problems. She is there as a facilitator who uses her skills to help her client find and use his own resources. Many individuals find that the questions a coach asks help them to understand their strengths and acknowledge their weaknesses. This process is helpful in building up self-confidence and a positive outlook.

Many benefits accrue to the company when trust has been established and individuals have an opportunity to air their difficulties. Often when an individual has the freedom to sound off and discuss ideas he makes excellent suggestions. Many cost-saving ideas and useful suggestions for efficient work practices come out of coaching.

PERSONAL DEVELOPMENT

Coaching techniques are powerful. They help clients identify and achieve goals and overcome obstacles that stop them. There is a widely held belief that coaching is only for problem employees or for dealing with problem issues. This is one of those urban myths that need to be shattered.

A wrong understanding of what happens in the coaching session can discourage executives from agreeing to participate. Nearly everyone can benefit if they are open to the process. Even the highest of high flyers can benefit from improving their communication skills. The spin-off benefits are improved relationships with colleagues and family and greater satisfaction in all aspects of life.

It cannot be emphasised enough that coaching is not therapy. It is not designed to deal with family problems or serious emotional issues. The purpose of coaching is to build on a person's strengths and identify their weaknesses. However it is not possible to focus only on the person's work-life.

A one-to-one coaching relationship will by its very nature involve attitudes, beliefs, feelings and relationships in the workplace and family. Personal issues will come up in particular contexts. If relationship problems do not have a direct bearing on the work situation it is appropriate for the coach to say when issues go beyond their area of expertise.

A coach is not there to intervene with management and at the first session clear guidelines need to be established and agreed. There are some issues that cannot be addressed in business coaching and would be more appropriately dealt with in counselling and therapy.

THE COACHING SESSION AT WORK

In the first coaching session the ground rules are set out.

When and where meetings occur, the duration and frequency of sessions are agreed and issues about confidentiality are discussed and clarified.

Good work will only take place when rapport is established and a supportive, safe and respectful environment is created.

Clear and specific goals and objectives will need to be put forward and the client will take responsibility for coming up with an action plan.

The coach's role will be to get commitment from the individual to follow the action plan and provide feedback about progress.

LOCATION

The coaching session should take place at the same time and in a location that is private and convenient for the coach and client. An office where the coach and client will not be disturbed or overheard is essential. The location of the office needs to afford privacy. Having a client walk through an open plan office to get to a coaching session is not helpful.

A neutral venue away from the office can work very well. The location of the session can have a very important bearing on the outcome. I hardly need to stress that the meeting space needs to be quiet without the interruption of telephones that need to be answered or people popping in to ask questions.

PARTICIPATIVE RELATIONSHIP

The effective business coach must have skills to elicit appropriate and helpful information about the issues that need to be addressed. Open-ended questions that require more than a 'Yes' or 'No' response challenge the client to clarify his own goals and objectives.

Some people are unhappy about how they are treated in the workplace but they have no clarity about the part they play in that problem. Questions that invite a person to become aware of what they are thinking and feeling can get them to express how they feel about issues and challenge them to make decisions on what action to take.

Discovering the negative self-talk that uncovers fear of failure is often all that is needed for a client to get out of a rut and become a productive member of staff. Coaching is a participative relationship which empowers a manager and staff to set specific goals that are realistic and achievable within a specified timeframe.

STYLES OF COACHING

There are different views regarding whether it is better for an Executive Coach to have a business background or not. Personally I don't think it matters. The client always has the answers. A lack of knowledge can even prove an asset. Often when an executive has to explain what he means without using jargon it clarifies why mis-understandings occur.

Words are only a small part of communication. When a client is put in a position where he has to explain the technical terms he normally uses in simple language his coach will get many opportunities to watch how he responds in situations that are unfamiliar.

In every form of coaching the client is challenged to become aware of his own emotional responses and body language. A man who is focused on his intellectual strengths and weaknesses and out of touch with his feelings is out of balance. He may achieve brilliant results at work but other areas of his life will be unfulfilling. The coach can challenge him to identify what is behind that lack of fulfilment. Usually it's fear that inhibits him from reaching his full human potential.

The advantages of dealing with fear and identifying where it comes from are numerous. The benefits include more self-awareness, enhanced self-confidence and more balance in every area of life. Coaching will have a very positive effect in helping staff improve their performance, develop self-belief and keep focused on achieving the goals they set.

DIFFERENT APPROACHES

The Sounding Board approach to coaching is quite different from the task-focused approach. There are many situations when an individual is faced with choices and simply needs to sound off to explore the consequences of those choices in order to make a decision. People who have relationship issues with their colleagues need to give vent to their feelings in order to clarify for themselves what action to take.

Often problems are quickly resolved when the client feels heard. It's incredible how often conflict situations are amicably sorted. The coach simply listens in a respectful way, reflects back what she is hearing and shows that she understands the problem. The coach is not there to solve problems but to facilitate individuals in finding their own solutions. Most clients who feel heard when they sound off will find a workable solution.

Task-focused coaching is effective with a client who has a clear idea of what he wants to accomplish. Staff members who have goals that are clearly defined can often find when they work with a coach that their expectations are unrealistic. They may decide to delegate when they recognise how they put themselves under stress by attempting to do too much.

Stress due to time management problems is common. Some managers set goals that involve a whole team and live with enormous tension when members of the team fail to deliver on time. Learning a new strategy of setting goals for only the tasks he fully controls can make a huge difference to stress levels and to the performance of others. People become responsible when they are given responsibility.

Coaching is all about empowering the client to get in touch with the vast reservoir of untapped talents that he is not using. The process that works with an underachiever and motivates him to unlock his potential will also work with the high flyer. The underachiever may have come with excellent people skills and poor job prospects. The high flyer may come with a brilliant job but have poor people skills.

Both need to focus on identifying what is working well and to change what's not working. The benefits of working with a coach who has a holistic approach is that whatever issues are brought to coaching are dealt with in the context of the whole person. The mentoring relationship is incredibly effective in helping clients improve every area of their lives.

Coaching is as effective with the struggling sales manager trying to meet his targets as it is with the successful team leader who is looking for new challenges.

SUMMARY

- **Bullying in the workplace.**
- **One-to-one support.**
- **Communication skills.**
- **Strategies for communication.**

'If you are not investing at least 10% of your gross income (and preferable of your desired income) in your knowledge, know-how, training and conditioning, via books, tapes, newsletters, seminars, coaching and consulting, I think you are incapable of sustaining a high performance'.

DAN KENNEDY

Bibliography

Alder, H, & Heather, B., NLP in 21 Days, Judy Piatkus Publishers, London, 1999

Allen, R.P., Scripts and Strategies in Hypnotherapy, Vol 1, Crown House Publishing, Carmarthen, 1997

Andreas, S. & Faulkner, C., NLP The New Technology of Achievement, Nicholas Brealey Publishing, London, 1996

Andreas, Connirae Ph. D. and Andreas Steve MA. Heart of the Mind: Engaging your Inner Power to Change with Neuro Linguistic Programming. Moab, Utah: Real People Press 1989

Andreas, Connirae PhD and Andreas Steve MA. Change you Mind-And Keep the Change. Moab, Utah: Real People Press 1987

Andreas, C. & Andreas, T., Core Transformation: Reaching the Wellspring Within, Real People Press, Moab Utah, 1994

Bandler, R. & McDonald, W., An Insider's Guide to Sub-Modalities, Meta Publications, Capitola CA, 1988

Bandler, Richard and Grinder, John. Using your brain for a CHANGE; Moab, Utah: Real People Press 1987.

Bandler, R. & Grinder, J., Frogs into Princes, Neuro Linguistic Programming Real People Press, Moab Utah, 1979

Bandler, R. & Grinder, J., The Structure of Magic 1, Science and Behavior (Sic) Books, Palo Alto CA, 1975

Bandler, R. & Grinder, J., The Structure of Magic, Volume 2,: Science and Behavior Books, Palo Alto, CA

Bandler, R. & McDonald, W., An Insider's Guide to Sub-Modalities, Meta Publications, Capitola CA, 1988

Battino, R. & South, L., Ericksonian Approaches, Crown House Publishing, Carmarthen, 1999

Best, Lang, Lodge Dunaway, Watkins. Pastoral Care and Personal Cassell Social Education. Cassell, London 1995

Bloom, Allan. Love and Friendship

Bradbury, A., Develop Your NLP Skills, Kogan Page, London, 2000

Bradshaw, John. Family Secrets: Bantam 1995

Bradshaw, John. Homecoming. Piatkus Houston, USA 1990

Bradshaw, John. The Family: HCI 1988

Bradshaw, John. Healing the Shame that Binds You: Binds You: HCI 1988

Breemen S.J., Peter G. van. As Bread That Is Broken: Dimension Books

Bodenhamer, B.G. & Hall, L.M., The User's Manual For The Brain, Crown House Publishing, Carmarthen, 1999

Cameron-Bandler, L., Solutions; Enhancing Love, Sex and relationships, Real People Press, Moab, Utah, 1985

Cameron-Bandler, L. & Lebeau, M., The Emotional Hostage, Real People Press, Moab, Utah, 1986

Chopra, Deepak. Unconditional Life. New York: Bantam Books 1991.

Corey, C. Theory and Practice of Counselling and Psychotherapy, (6th Edit)Wadsworth, London 2001

Culley, S., Integrative Counselling Skills in Action, Sage Publications, London, 1991

Davis Brigham, Deirdre, Imagery for Getting Well: New York: Norton 1996.

De Mello, Anthony S.J. Walking on Water: The Columba Press. 1992

DeLozier, J. & Grinder, R., Turtles all the way down, Grinder & Associates, CA, 1987

Egan, G, The Skilled Helper, (7th Edit) Brooks/Cole, Pacific Grove CA., 2001

Fridlund, Reisberg. 9.5 pt: Norton

Gibran, Kahlil, *The Prophet: Oneworld* Publications 1995

Gleitman, Fridlund, Reisberg. *Psychology*: Norton.

Goleman, Daniel. Emotional Intelligence: Bloomsbury

Gray, J., Men are from Mars, Women are from Venus, Thorsons, London, 1992

Gray, J., How to Get What You Want And Want What You Have, Vermillion, London, 1999

Hall, L. Michael and Bodenhaner, Bob. Figuring Out People: Design Engineering with Meta_Programs. Wales, United Kingdom: Crown House Publishing. 1997.

Hall, L. Michael and Bodenhaner, Bob. The User's Manual for the Brain: Wales, United Kingdom: Crown House Publishing. 2001

Harris, T.A., I'm OK, You're OK, Pan Books, London, 1973

Humphreys, Tony. Myself, My Partner: G.&M 1997.

Jung, Carl. Memories, Dreams and Reflections. New York: Random-Vantage, 1989.

LeCron, L.M., Self-Hypnotism, Signet, New York, 1970

McDermott, I. & O'Connor, J., Neuro-Linguistic Programming and Health, Thorsons, London, 1996

McHugh, R.P., Mind With a Heart, Gujarat Sahitya Prakash, India, 1998

Mulligan, Eileen. Life Coaching, Change your life in 7 days. London. Pitkus 1999.

May, Rollo. Freedom and Destiny: Norton

Nelson-Jones, R., Human Relationship Skills, Cassell, Eastbourne, 1986

McDermott, I. & O'Connor, J., Neuro-Linguistic Programming and Health, Thorsons, London, 1996

O'Connor, J., NLP Workbook, Thorsons, London, 2001

O'Connor , Jospeh and Prior, Robin. NLP & Relationships: Thorsons, London 2000.

O'Connor, J. & Seymour, J., Introducing NLP (2nd Edit) Thorsons, London, 1995

O'Connor, J. & Seymour, J., Training with NLP, Thorsons, London, 1994

Pease, Alan & Barbara., Why men don't listen and Women can't read maps, Pease Training International, Mona Vale NSW, 1999.

Powell, John S.J .The Secret of Staying in Love: Thomas More

Powell S.J. Unconditional Love: Thomas More

Powell, Brady. Will the Real me Please Stand Up:

Powell, John S.J. Why am I afraid to love: Thomas More

Powell, John S.J. Happiness is an inside job: Thomas More

Powell, John S.J. Fully Human, Fully Alive: Thomas More

Powell, John, S.J. Why am I Afraid to Tell You Who I Am? Thomas More

Prior, R. & O'Connor, J., NLP & Relationships, Thorsons, London, 2000

Richardson, Cheryl. Life Makeovers: Bantam Books

Robbins Anthony. Unlimited Power. The new Science of Personal Achievement.

Robbins Anthony. Awake the Giant Within. How to take control of your mental, emotional, physical and financial destiny. Simon & Schuster 1992.

Rogers, C. On Becoming a Person, Constable, London, 1961

Rosenthal, Don & Martha. Intimacy, The Nobel Adventure: Collins Press

Stevens, J.O., Awareness, Eden Grove Editions, London, 1989

Satir, V., Peoplemaking, Science and Behavior (Sic) Books, Palo Alto CA, 1972

Satir, Virginia. Making Contact. Berkley, California: Celestial Arts, 1976.

Sheehy,Gail. New Passages: Harper Collins

Skynner, Robin & Cleese,John, Life and how to Survive It: Vermillion

Stevens, J.O., Awareness, Eden Grove Editions, London, 1989

Tannen, Deborah. The Argument Culture. Virgo Press 1998.

Tannen, D., I Only Say This Because I Love You, Virago Press, London, 2001

Training International, Mona Vale NSW, 1999.

The New Oxford Dictionary, Oxford University Press, Oxford 2001

Vanzant Iyanla. In the meantime: Pocket Books

Winkelhuis, M., Dance To Your Maximum, Karstens, Leyden, 2001

Wynne, Carmel. Relationships and Sexuality, Dublin, Mercier :1997.

Wynne, Carmel. Sex and Young People, The Knowledge to Guide the Young People in Your Life. Dublin.. Mercier 2001.

Zagler, Zig. See you at the top. Gretna: Pelican Publishing Company. 1984

Zukav, Gary. The Seat of the Soul. New York: Simon & Schuster, 1989.

TEMPLATE OF WHEEL

This exercise will help you to identify priority areas that need your immediate attention.

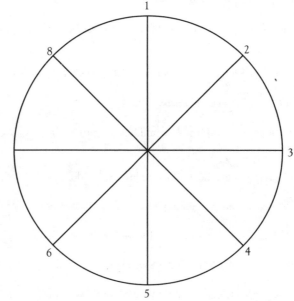

Directions:

Using the 'Wheel of Life' model, mark the segments of the wheel with your eight top priorities from the list below. Score your sense of satisfaction for each on a scale from 0 to 10. O is at the centre of the circle and 10 at the outer edge. The outer rim shows you are achieving satisfactorily.

Customer Services	Risk Taking
Strategic Planning	Team Development
Managing Change	Goal Setting
Results	Family
Communication	Fun and Recreation
Decision Making	Spirituality

NOTES

NOTES

NOTES

NOTES